Unexpected Conversations with Teenagers

A Spiritual Journey with Young Minds

Charles C. Ledbetter

Unexpected Conversations with Teenagers

Published by Ledbetter Land & Cattle Company

The incidents in this book appear essentially as I remember them; however the names and certain identifying features of some people portrayed have been changed to protect their privacy.

Editor: Karen Reddick, The Red Pen Editor
Cover and interior design: Rebecca Finkel, F + P Graphic Design
Photos: Charles C. Ledbetter

Newspaper clippings courtesy *The Denver Post,*
archived in the Denver Public Library, main branch.

Books may be purchased for educational and promotional use.
Please contact the author at
charlescledbetter.com

ISBN (softcover): 978-1-732-9339-0-3
ISBN (eBook): 978-1-732-9339-1-0

In memory of Alton R. Brown,
who put me on this path
and to teenagers of all ages;
particularly, the past, present,
and future teens of
Hope United Methodist Church.

Acknowledgments

My sincere thanks and gratitude go out to the following family, friends, savants, and all-around good folks. My wife, Sharon, for her infinite patience with me, not only during the process of writing this story, but since we first met, and for reading my first drafts and gently correcting my grammar and punctuation.

Jim Hankins, for the inspiration and encouragement to write this story and for introducing me to my editor, Karen Reddick. Ceil Cleveland, for reading my first draft and encouraging me to continue writing. A couple of renaissance men, Tom Miller and the Honorable James Patrick Vandello, for reading my early drafts and giving suggestions on structure and storytelling.

Shirley Meier, for her wise counsel and sage advice as this story took form. Anne Randolph, for her wisdom and advice in guiding me through the process of writing this story.

Rebecca Finkel, F + P Graphic Design for her professional ability and advice.

Janos Toevs, Dani Rowland, Aron Ralston, Linda Coughlin-Brooks, Kari Anderson Motz, Betsy and Cal Anderson, Courtney Anderson, and Bryce Harman for their permission to use parts of our shared experiences in this book. Mary Voss, daughter of Helen Gail Mangold, for permission to use part of her mother's life experiences and those with the teens of our class.

Contents

INTRODUCTION

Lunch with a Pastor

On a bright Sunday in April 1984, the warm spring weather pulled my thoughts away from church toward the snow-capped mountains visible in the distance. After the worship service, the senior pastor held my handshake for several seconds longer than usual. He leaned in and asked if we could have lunch the coming week because he wanted to discuss something with me.

The short conversation set off alarm bells in my mind. What could he possibly want? Did I do something to catch his attention? Before I got to my car, I formulated a plan to get my stewardship pledge up to date. It wouldn't be easy, but I thought I could do it. Things were a bit unsettled with me at the time. What I euphemistically called "exploring new opportunities" in my career created a bit of a cash-flow problem.

Eleven years practicing law, with varying degrees of financial success, brought me to this point. My dad, a district court judge, allowed me as a kid, to hang around the courthouse in my hometown. The small group of lawyers I observed while growing up came in the country lawyer stereotype of honest and hardworking people. They operated under the credo: a person's word is his bond. I found the 4,000 or so lawyers in my milieu quite different. Some years I flourished and found monetary success, but mostly I lived a month-to-month struggle to pay the bills. Most months I discussed my line of credit with the bank officer and hoped to meet payroll by month's end.

A few months before my encounter with the senior pastor, I began exploring the possibility of not practicing law, of changing careers. I sought a high-level sales job in the financial services industry working with wealthy individuals, foundations, endowments, and retirement plans. My legal experience, especially with ERISA, the Employee Retirement Income Security Act of 1974, helped me attract employers. Later, I used my expertise to build a career away from the practice of law.

When my lunch with the pastor came around, I held doubts about my future career plans. The luncheon served as a pleasant distraction from constantly thinking about other career prospects. The pastor motioned for me to sit down across from him in a booth. After sitting down, but before we settled in, the pastor cleared his throat and said, "I wanted to ask you something." He paused, took a breath, and slowly continued, "I believe you could become a terrific Sunday school teacher. Would you consider it?"

Nothing like getting right to the point. I didn't know what to say, so I remained quiet. I took my napkin and laid it across my lap, my mind racing for a response. A tightness gripped my stomach. No doubt, he saw the puzzled look on my face and quickly continued, "I've observed your interaction with people and believe you relate well to most folks. We need a senior high Sunday school teacher and I want you to do it."

I attended Hope United Methodist for the first time only a couple of years before this. How could this give him enough time to observe me interacting with others? Although flattered, I remained skeptical. He must be selling me something, or taking a leap of faith on someone he hardly knew. I wondered why.

"Me?" I managed to stammer. The conversation headed in a completely different direction from my prepared response about bringing my pledge giving up to date. After a few awkward moments of silence, I finally responded, "Senior high, teenagers, right?"

"Yes, typically fourteen to eighteen-year-olds, although sometimes we have a few younger and a few older. No college kids, grades 9 through 12. I am sure you can relate well to teenagers," he continued.

I tried to think of an intelligent response and not hurt the guy's feelings. Whatever I thought we might discuss this never occurred to me. I wiped a few drops of sweat from my forehead drawing a complete blank on what to say next. What I said next surprised even me, "Even though once a teenager myself, I am not sure I like them."

My sons were almost thirteen and eleven and I thought about how I communicated with them. It did not inspire confidence. No longer married, my sons lived with their mother, but I spent time with them most weekends and tried to attend most school and sports events. Despite these efforts, I hardly felt qualified to coach or mentor teenagers on anything, especially religion. Sure, I took religion courses in college and read a lot, although not all, of the standard Protestant Bible, but this made me no religious scholar. Besides, I rebelled against many of the "holier than thou" attitudes and manipulations I witnessed as a youth in church. I still held a grudge against a youth pastor who gathered all of us together during a Youth Camp and asked everyone who was "saved" to raise their hand. Most did, but some kids did not. The harsh focus embarrassed them. Of course, the youth leader overlooked this fact and wanted them to jump up and say they wanted to be saved. The memory disgusted me and I thought it grossly unfair. This struck me as coercion or intimidation.

In my view, something as serious as one's eternal salvation or a commitment to a religion should not come from a heavy-handed guilt trip. Somewhere I read about Emily Dickinson's painful experience at Holyoke Seminary. Girls in her group were asked to stand or march down front in the chapel and declare themselves for Jesus. Apparently, during this episode, at age sixteen, Emily Dickinson remained seated, the only one. She related to her friends "although you may have thought it queer I didn't stand, but I thought a lie would be queerer." Bully for her.

Besides, the Jesus I imagined would have no tolerance for such behavior. Surely, he would be disappointed if one's faith in him resulted from fear and intimidation. For me, long periods of prayer, study, and introspection led to such decisions, not some youth leader's pressure or embarrassment at a summer camp. I vowed this over enthusiastic worship practice could do without my participation.

"You have this wrong. I am no good at religious instructions according to John Wesley and the Methodist church. I don't believe in unscrewing the top of some kid's head and pouring into their brains a lot of religious mumbo-jumbo. I think they should learn to think for themselves," I heard myself say.

The pastor only grinned.

My confirmation and learning in the United Methodist church made me aware of the "Quadrilateral"– John Wesley's methodology for ascertaining what to believe. Its four corners are scripture, reason, experience, and tradition. While I studied some scripture and tradition in the Methodist church, I leaned toward the reason and experience pillars. I certainly could not give kids chapter and verse for the entire Bible. To my way of thinking, following a tradition alone, without serious consideration, did not make it imperative. Surely, once the pastor learned this, no way he would let me near young disciples.

"I don't want someone dictating to our youth," he said. "We need someone who can relate to them and answer their questions. It doesn't mean you will always have the right answer, but I believe you relate well to people and will treat them as individuals on their own spiritual journey. Young people need recognition, encouragement, and love. I am sure you can do it."

Pastors often say the right things at the right times and his next statement certainly got an unexpected response from me, "Well, if you are afraid . . ."

Let me first say; woe unto those who practice false bravado. I must have lost my mind for a second. I looked the pastor in the eye and said, "I have been struck by lightning (I didn't mention it happened while on an airplane), spent a hitch in the United

States Marine Corps, and the IRS audited my tax return. I am not afraid of anything. I'll do it."

I continued to wonder though why the pastor thought I could teach Sunday school for teens, and began to think about my experiences with young folks. Experience with my sons showed mixed results. Once I became so dissatisfied with the basketball coach at the YMCA league, I volunteered to coach the next year. We lost 11 of 12 games.

Other times, if I came home to find the room a shamble and the lamp busted, Mike would say Andy did it and Andy would say Mike did it. If I got both in the room, they said the dog did it. I would have to become Columbo the detective, Wapner the judge, and Torquemada the torturer all at the same time. Who said I lacked experience with young folks?

Perhaps the pastor knew about me teaching the boys about the omnipresence of God. Because they behaved themselves relatively well around parents or adults, I wanted to teach them God is always watching us wherever we may be. My goal became teaching them they came under the All Mighty's gaze even when alone.

To drive this point home, one time I pulled Andy in for a talk. I told him he needed to be a good boy even with no adults around. To cement the thought, I asked, "Do you know where God is?"

He did not respond and looked around the room as though he hoped an answer might come to him. I asked again, a little louder and with more force, "Do you know where God is?" He looked at me with utter confusion, scratched his chin a bit, but still no answer.

When I released him to rejoin his brother, I followed to listen. Mike said, "What's up with Dad?" Andy replied, "I'm not sure, but apparently God is missing, and Dad thinks we did it."

Whatever his reasons, the pastor became willing to trust me for an hour on Sunday mornings with a room full of teenagers. For the next thirty-three years, I held class for the senior high, but I hesitate to say I taught a class, as I certainly learned more from them than they ever learned from me. This gave me first-hand experience with many accomplished young people and many who remain under construction. So much so I began keeping lists of teens encountered during those thirty-three years. I made an A list for the accomplished folks and an under-construction list for those missing the mark. Regardless of the list one occupies, all are children of God and worthy of her love.

You may wonder why I refer to God with a female notion. Soon after agreeing to teach the class, I determined I would refer to God as female. I wanted partly to stir things up a tad by going against the generally accepted male role for God, but the other reason related to my thinking if God is omniscient and amazing beyond our comprehension, what does God need with a gender?

And, yes, those on the lists are all children of God, but more poignant and appropriate for this story, both the accomplished and the under-construction teenagers sat in the Sunday school class I led from 1984 to 2017.

The overwhelming majority of teens who sat in the class belong on the A list, and their parents should be proud, but I believe those under construction are like the lost sheep in Jesus' parable in the Gospel of Matthew 18:12-13: *What do you think? If a man owns a hundred sheep, and one of them wanders away, will he not leave the ninety-nine on the hills and go to look for the one that wandered off? And if he finds it, I tell you the truth, he is happier about that one sheep than about the ninety-nine that did not wander off.*

One can read the scripture to mean anyone who lost his way. Because I wanted to avoid contributing to anyone ending up permanently on the under-construction list, and following the pastor's suggestion, I sought to apply certain principles to reach teenagers.

First, I wanted to acknowledge them. To me, it meant expressing recognition of them, seeing them, talking to them. Too often adults pass by teens without acknowledging them, without speaking to them, just ignoring them. Some teens feel invisible because of this. Some act out to get attention. Acknowledging them first can head off a lot of this behavior.

Second, I sought to encourage them. They need seasoning, maturity, experience. Maybe we cannot open their heads and pour in wisdom, but we can encourage them to study, participate, question, and learn. Asking them what they think triggers an amazing interaction. Discussing issues works better than preaching to them. Letting them know we all are on a spiritual journey encourages them and validates their thoughts. Most importantly, I tried to be real with them. As dogs and horses can sense fear in humans, teens can sense hypocrisy a mile away. If you don't believe it, good luck selling it to them.

Finally, I tried to love them. This can be difficult, but it pays great dividends. Having teens know you love them and will not give up on them, goes a long way toward building lifetime relationships. At baptisms in the United Methodist church, the congregation affirms: With God's help we will so order our lives after the example of Christ, that this child, surrounded by steadfast love, may be established in the faith and confirmed in the way that leads to life eternal. Living into this affirmation requires effort, not lip service. I tried to live out those words with the teens in class.

As an example of this steadfast love, I remember a time a youth in the church bemoaned the fact both sides of his family ancestors lacked living grandparents. He saw other teens his age enjoying grandparents at games, activities, and holidays and missed this connection between generations. His mother mentioned this to another member of the congregation. The next Sunday, an older man who learned about it, approached the youth and volunteered he and his wife would act as the young man's grandparents.

They shook hands and for the next few years developed a strong and loving relationship. A few years later, the older man died, and the youth grieved as much as if he lost his maternal grandfather. Their relationship became a great example of loving someone and putting your actions where your heart is. Both the teen and the older man told everyone they received more from the relationship than they gave.

Not all of us are able to surround a teen with steadfast love like this example, but we can acknowledge them, encourage them, and show we love them. It's a start.

A word of caution: Pastors with lunch invitations can lead one down many unbelievable paths.

CHAPTER ONE

Pillow Fight

How did my thirty-three years of interaction with teens go? Within a few weeks of agreeing to work with senior high youth, an opportunity to interact with many of them on a mission trip came along. I lacked confidence, but I felt a week with teens should give me some time to relate.

The first day of the trip, I sat with the youth leader in the fresh mountain air near the top of Wolf Creek Pass. I hoped to get some pointers on relating to teenagers and used the quiet moment to approach the young lady. Being fifteen to twenty years younger, I doubted her wisdom, but hey, I needed all the help I could get. Besides, she completed a theology degree at the Iliff School of Theology. Surely, they taught her the secrets of being an effective leader or teacher of young people.

While we stared at the cool mountain stream bubbling over the rocks, I asked, "What's the secret of relating to the youth? While I have two sons, they are younger, and I don't have much experience with teens."

She seemed surprised I sought her advice. "Oh, I don't know. I have only been a youth leader for a little over a year." She responded with a little embarrassment. "This is my first real job with youth. I have mostly been a volunteer while I went to school."

Oh, great! I thought. What had I gotten myself into? Not only am I adrift, but I have a rookie to teach me.

"Be yourself, I guess," she finally answered. "Kids don't like phonies. They can spot them a hundred miles away."

Well, this helped, a little. I could be myself, but I still struggled with how I could be an effective teacher/mentor/supporter of young folks in a class setting at church.

After my not-so-enlightening conversation with the young youth leader, our band of senior high teens continued our trip south to a Navajo reservation in northern New Mexico for a week of work, fellowship, and outreach to the tribe.

Our church had a tradition of reaching out to the Native American people. This mission approach may have resulted from the terrible things done to the American Indians over the previous 150 years, including some by God-fearing, white, Methodist settlers who poured into the western states. The gesture could not erase the treatment of Native Americans in the nineteenth century, but it took a step in the right direction for these youths to do something for others not as fortunate.

I drove one of the vans and took responsibility for twelve youths. In those days, no one carried personal electronic devices so the kids sang and told jokes and stories all the way to the first stop. My ears rang with the chatter and sounds of teenagers.

On the way, we stopped at the Sand Dunes National Monument where I thought I might have time to interact with the youth, but after an hour exploring this national treasure, everyone feverishly brushed sand from clothes, hair, and body parts, and then reloaded into the vans. No incidents of trouble, but few interactions other than counting noses to be sure we left no one behind. No Bible lessons, no hymns, no speeches on the merits of Christian community service. I took the role of a glorified van driver.

Until this trip, my association with the youth only covered a few weeks. They were getting to know me while I got to know them. I led a few classes on Sunday mornings before this, but they were mostly get acquainted type sessions without a lot of structure or direction. So far, neither they, nor I, went out of our way to connect on a deeply personal basis. We had mostly polite interactions, but this would soon change.

We arrived in Durango, Colorado for our first night's stay. We reserved the basement of the local church for the boys, one father, and me. No coed sleeping arrangements for the Methodists. The girls stayed at an auxiliary building next to the church. Sleeping bags on the floors and a toilet. No showers or luxury accommodations for us.

After grabbing a bite at a fast food restaurant, the youth leader gathered all of us on the church lawn for a vesper service. We sat on the grass, sang some songs and talked about our upcoming mission to the Navajo tribe. Like many Native American people, they suffered from poverty, high rates of alcoholism, and chronic unemployment. Our youth came from middle to upper-middle class families and had issues, but not the same ones the Navajo youth faced. She cautioned about making a big deal about us helping them. She recommended a silent or quiet disciple approach. I admit, I secretly wondered how the kids and our leaders would react to the challenge.

After the service, the teens retired to their respective sleeping areas. The leader, the father of one of the youth, and I remained on the grass to visit and plan our next day's journey. Heading south to Farmington, New Mexico, and then to the reservation, we planned to arrive at our destination mid to late morning. Then, I headed for the basement to arrange my sleeping bag while the father and leader continued to talk.

Grabbing a cold sip from the water fountain at the top of the stairs, I heard a commotion in the basement. Not thinking much about it, but curious, I headed down. As I came through the door, a pillow smashed into my face. I staggered a little and looked shocked. Everyone froze. All eyes were on me and sparkled with anticipation of how I would react. I gathered myself, calmly walked to my bedroll, pulled out my pillow and smacked the closest teen I could find. The fight erupted!

This continued for several minutes until most of us were exhausted. I got in some good licks but took a few myself. After the fracas quieted down, one young man, one of the smartest of the group and a graduating senior, came over and sat down by me. "Everyone loved the pillow fight. Thanks for being a sport." He smiled and told me some of the boys changed their opinion of me after the fight. They apparently thought me being a lawyer and all, I fit the stereotype of a law and order type and would not cotton to any horseplay. Now, they thought I might be okay.

I passed the early test of acceptance and luckily, no one suffered a broken nose or a blinding poke in the eye. I wondered what I might do when I needed to discipline them or assert the parent/mentor role. A Sunday school teacher's job description surely did not include disciplinarian. Boy, did I have a lot to learn. I might not have this Sunday school teacher's role down pat, but I knew how to join a pillow fight.

The next morning at breakfast, the boys shared with the girls a blow-by-blow description of the pillow fight. Telling the tale with excited voices, they prominently mentioned my name as the chief pillow swinger, if not chief instigator of the fight. More than one sentence in the retelling included, "And then, Charlie …" The boys clearly made the case I took part with vigor and relish. I feigned complete innocence while flashing a big grin. Maybe this would also affect how the girls viewed me. Time would tell.

We arrived at the Navajo reservation a little after noon on Saturday amid blistering heat and little humidity. We met our liaison from the tribe, a dark-haired, high-cheek-boned Navajo woman about fifty years old. She showed us our quarters, an old, drafty, and stiflingly hot gymnasium. We dropped our bedrolls and backpacks and headed to lunch in the school cafeteria. After bologna and cheese sandwiches and cherry Kool-Aid, we gathered in the gym for an orientation lesson. The Navajo woman reiterated what the youth leader told us about chronic unemployment, alcohol abuse, and dysfunctional family dynamics among the tribe and told us not to expect a warm and friendly reception, especially from the adults. She thought the children and youth we encountered would welcome us, maybe as oddities for their amusement, or perhaps as curiosities. She indicated most on the reservation held no religious affiliation and would probably show little tolerance for proselytizing. Fine with me. I did not want to be an evangelist anyway.

Sunday would be a day of rest and games while we became acquainted with some of the Navajo youth. Monday the work would get underway.

After lunch, we unloaded the rest of our things from the vans and settled in. I noticed some of the kids worked hard, took direction, followed their own initiative, and generally made themselves valuable members of the team. Others sat by themselves or with a few friends and watched. I did not feel confident enough to tell them to get busy helping us, but I wondered how some jumped in and helped while others sat and watched.

On Sunday morning, I gave the boys a pep talk about being a team player and pitching in to help with tasks. I felt a fear of being branded a slacker or called lazy as a teen, but I quickly saw not all shared this attitude. Teens I encountered over the next thirty-three years fell into the same patterns. Some were doers and some were watchers. Most doers become accomplished citizens, while others remained under construction.

During the week, the youths worked hard and seemed to enjoy working with the Native American kids. In the mornings, we conducted a makeshift Vacation Bible School, acting out several bible stories for the kids. The afternoons were spent cleaning, painting, and repairing some of the housing on the reservation. The most excitement came one afternoon while a group of boys stacked and cleared a brush pile. One boy, a 200-pound football player at Overland High School, ran screaming from the site, clearly in a panic. The youth leader and I ran over to help. Turned out, a small spider and its web pushed this gentle giant's adrenalin into overdrive and away he went.

The night's devotional included the biblical admonishment: Fear Not. The group agreed this probably did not apply to spiders, and maybe snakes.

Soon the mission ended, but I did accomplish some things. I contributed one capable van driver, an adult to keep things on schedule, and a first-class pillow fighter. Most of all, I felt better about working with the youth and how they tentatively accepted me. I looked forward to how our relationships might develop.

Author, front row left, with Mission Team

The young man who came over to tell me joining the pillow fight enhanced my standing with the teenage boys? Years later after graduating Michigan University with a degree in Sociology, he became the executive director of a homeless shelter and HIV/AIDS Clinic in San Francisco, California. Definitely an accomplished person. And, the fellow scared of the spider? He became an engineer working on projects around the world, including some third world locations, where I am sure spiders proliferate. This fear did not keep him from the A list.

CHAPTER TWO

Charlie's Rules of Order

The youth group took the rest of the summer off without holding a formal Sunday school class. Other than a couple of evening gatherings to eat ice cream and talk about the mission trip, the group did not have a class until school started in late August. This gave me some time to figure out how to conduct a class. I tried to remember classes from my high school years but came up with little.

During my teen years, a girlfriend, Betsy, provided the biggest reason for going to the youth class and evening social gatherings. Smart, attractive, and full of life, she attracted boys easily. This green-eyed, blond-haired beauty became a faithful participant in our local church, so I showed up regularly too, mostly to see her. She liked me, but never missed an opportunity to poke fun of me, especially when I became a little full of myself. Remembering those pleasant memories of going to church to be around an attractive girl did not help much in formulating a plan to gain attention of teens and keep them interested in coming to class though.

Sure enough, the pastor asked me my plans for the fall classes. When I told him I struggled trying to figure out a process or some rules to follow, he told me we needed some rules and process, but he urged me to talk with the class and let things develop. The pastor made it sound a lot easier than anything my poor imagination produced up to that point.

With two years in the Marines and a law school degree, I knew rules, regulations, chain of command, and structure. Of course, the senior pastor took ultimate responsibility, but he gave me carte blanche to develop structure and format for holding a class for teens. What should I do? Establish Charlie's Rules of Order? Make a list of guidelines for all to follow? If the good Lord only gave Ten Commandments, maybe those would work for class. On the other hand, Deuteronomy seemed to add thousands of rules as the Hebrew children matured and multiplied, surely, our class could get by with fewer rules.

The few early classes were noisy and without structure. The kids talked among themselves and often ignored the lesson and me. Holding their attention became a challenge. At first, I chalked it up to my lack of experience and a game plan, but I soon realized mostly they liked it. Remembering my interest in seeing and talking to Betsy at church made me realize the behavior was typical. Many were interested in socializing or being around someone they liked, like me at the same age, instead of digging into lessons for a spiritual journey. Still, it bothered me and I wanted a way to keep a modicum of control in the class.

One night, an idea came to me. Since 1968, the official symbol for the United Methodist Church is the standard cross, but with two flames attached to the left as one faced the cross. The cross of course, the centuries old reminder of Jesus' sacrifice for humanity and a link to God through Christ. The United Methodist Church added the flames as a symbol of the Holy Spirit, or God's presence alive within each of us. The flames echo the story of Pentecost told in Acts of the Apostles where witnesses reported unity with the Holy Spirit and seeing "tongues of fire" descending from the sky. The two flames show the union of the two denominations, the Evangelical United Brethren Church and the Methodist Church, forming the United Methodist Church.

The flame from the Methodist cross and flame symbol gave me an idea for *Rule 1: Acknowledge God's presence.*

"What would you think if we lit a candle before starting each class?" I broached an idea with the class.

"Cool, can we have really big candles? I think lots of candles would be really *cool*." One responded.

"Does this mean we won't play any games? You know, where we might knock over a candle?" Another seemed disappointed.

"Here's what I have in mind. We use a candle flame to remind us of God's presence," I said somewhat reverently.

Next class I brought and prominently placed a candle on the table between the youth and me. I reminded them, well, actually informed them about the United Methodist Church symbol and trademark because they had no idea why the flame appeared on the symbol, and I stressed the part about the Holy Spirit being God's presence with us.

I sought out the oldest person in the room, myself excluded, to light the candle after we took attendance and collected an offering. This created some talk among the class as to birthday dates in what month and allowed some bonding. Maybe a formal ritual of lighting a candle would add some solemnity to the gathering. I thought the oldest, typically a senior in high school, might show more maturity and model good behavior for the others to follow.

Turned out getting a teenager, even one of the older ones, to light a candle with a match can turn into quite an exhibition. We used a big round candle several inches in diameter. These made great candles, but with repeated lightings, they burn a pit about two inches across and the wick becomes deeper and deeper from the top edge. Holding a match to reach the wick can prove problematic. Sometimes the person doing the lighting would blow it out inadvertently, requiring a re-striking of the matches, and often, the one lighting the candle would burn some fingers when the match burned down to the nub without lighting the wick.

A few years passed before I wised up and brought a fire-starter lighter, one of those with lighter fluid, a start button, a trigger, and a handle extending several inches away from the flame. No big requirements, simply hold down the button and squeeze the trigger. Voila, we created flames and no more burned fingers.

This generally worked better but created some funny moments when the less coordinated experienced trouble holding the trigger and pressing the start button at the same time. You have heard the saying about not being able to "walk and chew gum at the same time?" The principle goes double for teens operating a lighter and a simple candle.

Turned out the older ones did like the recognition and acknowledgement, so I continued to call on them to lead the opening of class. I heard some of the juniors and sophomores talk about when it would be their turn to light the candle. Most of the time we got it done, but a couple of missed attempts prompted sarcastic applause from the class when we finally lit the candle. I also naively thought reminding them of God's presence with us would put a damper on chitchat and goofing off. Instead, they acted pretty much as before despite Rule 1. So much for adding solemnity to the process.

Have you ever listened to a teenager talk? It takes some patience and wisdom to understand what they mean versus what they say. "Like," "You Know," and "Totally" get used a lot, but typically mean nothing. This led to *Rule 2: Do not start a sentence with "um."*

Toastmasters International Club taught me to avoid using verbal fillers or connectors such as um, uh, er, ah, like, okay, right, and you know. This also became a pet peeve of mine. When I heard someone start a sentence with um, it jarred me like the proverbial nails on the chalkboard sound. When one presents a speech to the Toastmasters' group, the Speech Master for the day listens intently and whenever the speaker uses a filler, he hits a bell—like those placed on the front desk of hotels in the old movies. The high-pitched bell sound interrupts everything and typically stops the speaker in his or her tracks. Soon even first-time speakers become painfully aware of the habit and learn to pause silently instead of adding those fillers.

Most teens, from my experience, are terrible about this habit. First, they talk fast. Next, they use many slang and semi-sentence phrases that mean something to them and their friends, but not to others. Finally, they are not trained speakers and generally do not think much before they speak. Like most of us, with practice and some experience, teens will improve their speech to the point of using complete sentences and the ability to convey cogent thoughts.

I started interrupting anyone who started a sentence with um. At first, they took offense, but later came to expect it. A funny thing happened. Often they stopped, paused, appeared to think, and then said um again. This typically brought laughter from the rest of us. It became a standing joke with the youth.

I told them someone trained former president Ronald Reagan to say "well" instead of um. Reagan often started sentences with "Well . . ." and then the rest of his thought. It gave the appearance of thinking and being careful about what he said, even though what followed might not make sense to anyone but him. I also told them saying well at least gives the impression you are thinking and lends a dramatic pause to your speaking. This usually holds an adult's attention.

My lectures and insistence on no ums intimidated one youth pastor so much when she came to deliver a sermon to the full church; she froze upon seeing me in the audience and stumbled through the sermon. She later said she lived in fear of me stomping my foot or slapping my hand on a table, to interrupt her if she said um.

After a few Sundays it became clear some of the teens attended class only because their parents made them. These captive audience members resented the class and took delight in disrupting it or causing as much mischief as possible. Some parents dropped their teens off at church for the senior high class and then went for coffee before returning at the end of class, although some parents attended classes themselves. Those attending because their parents required it led me to *Rule 3: You do not have to be here, regardless of what your parents said.*

My judgment felt it better to have a reasonably cooperative class than to spend forty-five minutes fighting with a disruptive teen and fifteen minutes trying to work with the rest of the class. When students acted up in class, I talked calmly to them in front of the class, telling them their actions made the class unproductive and I could not allow such. If that did not solve the problem, and sometimes it would not, I asked them to step outside the class for a private conversation.

Once outside the hearing of the class, I told them my solution. As a solution, I suggested they leave. If they did not want to be there, I did not want them there either. This approach set them back. Often, they were disbelieving they could leave. The thought never occurred to them. I would say, "Look, you will soon be eighteen and making decisions that carry far-reaching effects. You might as well start now. I will cover for you if your parents inquire, but frankly, I am doing you no good and you make me angry by your behavior, so let's agree on a solution. A good solution to my way of thinking is, you remove yourself from a situation you don't enjoy, and the rest of us continue with class."

This rule created an unholy alliance between those required to be in class and me. If a teen, who by mutual agreement with me, sat outside class in another part of the church building, received a challenge by the parents, I agreed to have their back.

I candidly told such teens I would cover for them so long as they did not create mischief in other areas of the church. If a parent called me, I would say I saw them on Sunday, a version of the truth, but one I could comfortably tell.

I only recall one instance where I needed to respond to a parent's direct question about someone being in class on Sunday. I responded with the truth but softened it some by saying they came to class, but we decided leaving worked okay for everyone. Rule 3 surprisingly produced good results. I thought many parents felt they did their part by getting their children to class, no need to further check on their attendance.

Once teens figured out I would not tolerate them disrupting the class and gave them a reasonable alternative, they often calmed down and went back to class. Some spent a Sunday or two by themselves and decided they liked it better to be with their friends, even if the price tag included listening to a lesson during the hour. Besides, they heard things about class and it made them sorry they missed something.

To others, this raised their opinion of me. If I accepted a role as their partner in crime for skipping class, I must not be a complete ogre. Some dropped out completely, never returning. This often resulted when the parents lost interest in bringing them to church or attending themselves. Others quietly rejoined our class.

One young man only attended our class twice. His parents dropped him off and returned an hour later. The second time we discussed Rule 3 and he left right away. Months later, I learned of his probation for illegal possession of firearms. He soon ran off to become involved with a Wiccan cult in Indiana. Many spend weeks, months, and maybe years under construction.

And then we get to Janos.

CHAPTER THREE

A Boy Interrupted

My questions to a first-time attendee seemed reasonable to me. We took roll and wrote down the names and phone numbers for the class members, first for the church's records and next for my often-forgetful memory. Meeting a teen one week and not being able to call them by name the next, irritated me most. To cover for this, I often joked about being older and forgetful, but I wanted to do better. How many of us, when introduced to someone, two minutes later find we cannot recall his or her name? Me, too.

"What is your name and phone number?" I asked the teen standing in front of me.

"Why do you need this information?" he asked.

"I keep track of class members for the church records and for me to learn everyone's name," I looked down at my note pad, ready to write his name.

"I promise you will remember my name, and it is an invasion of my privacy to collect a phone number," he looked me straight in the eye with no hint of a smile.

Taken aback and unsure what to say next, I paused for several seconds. Thinking on it more, the challenge merited a longer pause, but I finally said, "We need phone numbers to contact your parents in case of an emergency." Sounded good to me. Not Janos.

"I am Janos, which is John in eastern European languages, Edwards Toevs, the Fourth! I am not a junior, or a third, but a fourth. You surely can remember that, and I am NOT giving you a phone number. My parents adopted me, and frankly, could not care if I disappeared in a tornado. Got it?" He blurted out with some added vehemence. He then smiled, but sounded a defiant, even angry, tone. This mystified me and I wondered about his parents, or as he put it, his adoptive parents. I knew his mother played bridge with one of the pillars of the church and his father worked as a business executive. Nothing in this background gave me pause or made me think the parents uncaring.

Janos, slightly built, measured five-foot five inches, and weighed about 110 pounds. When we first met, I looked at a typical sixteen-year-old sophomore at Cherry Creek High School with acne and a gangly appearance. He came with a reputation for intelligence and a snarly attitude toward anyone in authority. I later learned his IQ topped 160 and it came with an attitude off the charts. I knew no other teen like him, at Hope church, or anywhere, then or since.

I stand six-foot one inch and weigh around 175 pounds, heavier and certainly taller than most teenagers. The height advantage gave me a commanding physical presence with teens, even if inside I lacked confidence. Hovering over a five-foot five-inch fourteen-year-old gave me an eight-inch advantage. For some teens, looking up at me while we talked proved intimidating enough, especially if I closed the personal distance between us to less than a foot. When seeking to control the class, or more likely, one of the class members, I used this advantage on more than one occasion. This approach did not work with everyone as I soon learned. My lack of experience and confidence would soon be tested.

I decided to let his recalcitrance go and get on with the class. The Sunday lesson dealt with God providing guidelines for living, in this case the Ten Commandments, from the book of Exodus. I barely began when Janos interrupted. "Why not start with Genesis, it's the book before Exodus, and tell us about Onan spilling his seed on the ground? Sex and masturbation are topics all the boys in here can identify with."

Dumbstruck, I did not know where all this came from. Masturbation? The top five hundred things I planned to discuss with the class did not include this. It dawned on me I faced a well-read boy who possessed a scary intelligence. Did such a story exist? Probably a bluff. I tried to ignore him by saying, "Janos, that can be a topic for another day. Today we are talking about the Ten Commandments. These are God's rules given to the early Jews, about how they should live. They were her chosen people. God wanted them to act accordingly as they grew from a tribe into a nation."

I tried to get back to the topic at hand when Janos chimed in again. "Well, if you want to talk about Jewish identity and nation building in the Old Testament, you should talk about why God thought it important Onan help his brother's widow have children. A brother whose brother died must marry the widow and have sex with her so she could bear more children. Following this rule, the tribe could increase. Only problem, doing so cut Onan's share of the inheritance. So, Onan did what they call coitus interruptus, spilling his semen on the ground instead of into the widow, to avoid impregnating her. That's why God killed him."

Most of the class tittered at Janos' words and some held their hands over their mouths, in shock at Janos' outburst. Within less than a minute, he highjacked the class. They looked at me with anticipation of my next move. Janos put me in a jam. He smiled and waited.

No sixteen-year-old I knew could outline an obscure Old Testament story, discern God's purpose in it, and effectively explode an M-80 firecracker in class, all within the first minutes of the class. Maybe I could invoke Rule 3: if you don't want to be here, you don't have to be here, and, if he went for it, save myself from further embarrassment. However, it looked like Janos thoroughly enjoyed the class and intended to stay. How could I get him away from the class, or get him to shut up?

"Janos, could we discuss this outside, in the hallway?" I stammered.

He followed me out. The class's eyes followed us out the door as though the fight between the mongoose and the cobra moved outside their view. I felt like the cobra, much bigger and stronger, but ill prepared for the battle. Little did I know Janos had immunity from authority as the mongoose did from cobra venom. Besides, the quickness and nimbleness of Janos, like the mongoose, easily overcame my supposed advantages of size or age.

"Look, you can't interrupt the class like this. It is disrespectful to the others and to me. I prepared a lesson and want to get through it, but I can't, if you keep interrupting." I stretched into my utmost towering height, closed the distance between us to inches from Janos' face, and used my most adult sounding voice with perfect logic. Surely, I could regain control of the situation.

Janos stood ready, clearly more adept at arguing than I. Even though I argued for a living during my twelve years as a lawyer, I found myself out of my league. Oh, to be in front of a jury, laying out my case. Piece of cake compared to dealing with this teenager. Besides, juries do not interrupt and challenge everything you say. Janos did not follow the rules. I later learned Janos thought rules existed for others, not him.

"It is not disrespectful to add cogent points to your lesson about how God wants his people to live their lives. Besides, my contributions to class got a better reception than yours. It is more disrespectful for you to come into class totally unprepared, than for me to add some intelligence to the conversation," he calmly replied.

I could not think of anything else right then, but Janos only hesitated a second.

"Besides, you know each boy in the class masturbates, but you are afraid to discuss it. What kind of teacher are you? If we cannot discuss such things at church, what does it say about the church? Narrow-minded, closed to discussion, and intolerant! Does that represent the kind of church you have here?"

"The point is you are disrupting the class." I felt my pulse in both temples as my heart began to race. My thoughts became scattered as I felt the anger rising in me.

Janos continued with a big grin on his face. He obviously loved this. "The point? Are you qualified to teach this class? That's the point. You don't even know the classic Rabbinical interpretation of the story, the Christian apologists' ideas on the Onan story, the Roman Catholic Church's rule of forbidding sex except for procreation, the supposedly modern view toward sexuality of the Protestant Reformation, or even John Wesley's idea you could lose your soul by wasting the precious fluids meant for procreation. Why don't you discuss those things? Because you are too ignorant for the discussion."

At this point, I lost my temper and grabbed Janos as I forced my hands under his armpits and lifted him off the ground. With his slight weight, I raised him easily. For good measure, I slammed him against the wall. He grinned at me. "Stop it! You can't do this. You cannot interrupt the class and be such a wise-ass." I briefly wondered who could hear me as I yelled at Janos. "You need to leave and stay out of class unless you can behave yourself." I am sure I sounded like an irate parent more than a Sunday school teacher. I lost control.

After a few seconds, I lowered him until his feet touched the floor and took away my hands. I stared at him. He stared back at me with a silly grin. My hands trembled and my stomach twisted as though a bowl of spoiled potato salad rotted within.

"Go, and don't come back until you can behave." I left him in the hallway, went into the class, and closed the door behind me.

The charts for acceptable Christian behavior did not include my behavior, but he pushed me past my wit's end. What happened to love your enemies and turn the other cheek? Janos embarrassed me, provoked me with only a few interactions, and clearly enjoyed every minute of it. I thought once this got around the church, my teaching days would be over. No excuses. Embarrassment overcame me because of the way I attempted to handle Janos. Why did I allow him to provoke me?

No one said a word, but the expressions said it all. What happened? Where is Janos? My palms were sweaty and I continued breathing hard. Instead of enjoying a class of teenagers, I felt like I survived a mugging. In some ways, I had, but barely, and at great loss to my self-respect and confidence.

"The things Janos said, is that story in the Bible?" someone asked.

"Frankly, I am not sure. I do not know but will look it up. Anyway, it became clear to me Janos did not want to be here, so I asked him to leave and not come back."

"Next week, too?" Another ventured.

"Not unless he agrees to behave. He really upset me. I am sorry I lost my temper."

Sure enough, the pastor soon heard I threw Janos out of class and called me. I apologized profusely and tried to explain he provoked me and I lost my temper. The pastor showed understanding and patience, simply asked me to pray for patience. Oh, yeah, and try to control my emotions with the class. He did chuckle at Janos' reference to Onan and the spilling of his seed.

"He sure knows his Bible stories. We do not teach that one at Vacation Bible School, so I am not sure where he learned it. It is a tough discussion for teens; I can see how you might be flummoxed a bit." Thank goodness, our discussion ended at this point and the pastor let it go.

Janos came back to class only one time and behaved well. He interrupted a couple of times but lacked the anger and assertiveness he showed before. Mostly, he grinned at me as though he knew a secret, my incompetence as a Sunday school teacher.

Of course, I redoubled my efforts to keep cool in class, no matter how infuriating the behavior. Often, telling the story of throwing Janos out of class, and then relating what happened afterwards, headed off intemperate behavior by me or any class member.

As for Janos, the story told is he ran away from home later in the year and lived on the streets hustling drugs, sex, and conning people. His superior brainpower made most street people easy prey for his manipulations. He ingratiated himself to a reclusive genius whose superior intellect limited his acquaintances. Janos lived with him for a while and conned a $10,000 inheritance from him under the pretense he could triple the investment, supposedly by selling drugs on the street. Despite this person's intelligence, Janos suckered the money out of him. A few weeks later Janos moved out of the residence and began evading communication with him. Fearful Janos no longer had the money, the man pressured him to give it back. Truth be told, the money disappeared with no chance of any triple amount Janos promised. The standoff continued for a few weeks until the night of June 4, 1989, when Janos lured him to a secluded spot along the Cherry Creek jogging path in southeast Denver. There, a jury later determined, Janos beat him severely with a baseball bat and repeatedly plunged a butcher knife into his chest, killing him.

At twenty years of age, Janos received a life sentence for first-degree-murder, with a minimum of forty years in the Colorado Department of Corrections, before being eligible for parole.

For over three decades, Janos held the distinction of being the only one I threw out of Sunday school class. Years later, the incident became a cautionary tale told freshmen and repeated for older classmates any time someone disturbed the class.

Because the kids became familiar with me kidding around and making outlandish statements to catch their attention, many did not believe this story until I showed newspaper clippings and photos of Janos.

A twenty-year-old sentenced to life imprisonment in the Colorado Department of Corrections for murder? A life under construction. Several years passed before our paths crossed again.

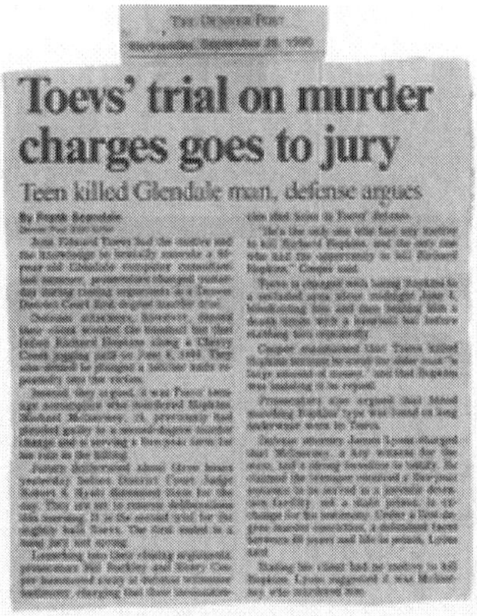

The Denver Post

Toevs' trial on murder charges goes to jury

Teen killed Glendale man, defense argues

John Toevs found guilty in murder

Life sentence for offense mandatory

CHAPTER FOUR

Social Principles

Our society forces many bad influences on young people. Sex, Drugs and Rock & Roll bedeviled the youth of the twentieth century, and although those pressures still exist today, new and powerful ones came with technology and the Internet. I never faced sexting, at sixteen or sixty.

I determined kids needed to be grounded in some beliefs and standards to help deal with these influences. I felt they needed something to stand for, but how to help teens without turning off many of them with the holy roller path of a pious, God-fearing disciple? This became my challenge. A heavy-handed religious dictate rarely worked for me. I wanted them to think for themselves, not parrot something I said, and if possible, have fun doing it. Thinking about how to live our lives, and what we believe in, presented ideas on engaging the class, but first I needed to get them talking to me. Getting and keeping a focus on our discussions continued as a challenge. The class liked to talk, but sometimes talking became a cacophony instead of a directed conversation.

As I continued gaining confidence teaching the class, getting everyone in class involved remained important to me. Some teens talked eagerly and quickly, others needed encouragement or cajoling to join into discussions. Following my tenet of acknowledging them, I made a point of addressing a question to each member of the class each time we got together. Often, I went around the room calling on each person in turn. Sometimes, I jumped around trying to address everyone while keeping them off guard. When jumping around the class, I learned to enlist the group by asking whom I missed. They invariably indicated those missed, wanting to spread to everyone the pain of being called upon.

Here my law training helped. Getting a witness, especially an uncooperative or adversarial one, to help your case is an art. Teens often resemble adversarial witnesses. I learned a few ways to generate a response, something to get us going. I asked a question. Some teens responded with a terse "I don't know," the perfect set up. I followed up with, "What do you think?" Challenging them to come up with something. I doubt the teens were flattered by my asking what they thought. Probably more annoyed, but at least I acknowledged them and encouraged them to speak their minds.

After a few times, they learned I would wait until they responded. If the question related to a number, distance, quantity, or such, and I got the "I don't know" response, I jumped in with an exaggerated number or answer and asked again.

An example might be the date for writing the New Testament. When the non-response came, I might ask, "Was it written in 1800 or 1950?" They knew those dates were wrong and generally started a discussion. Another example asked the language of the original New Testament writings. I would suggest English, Spanish, or Chinese, followed by a rolled eye response, but it got them thinking. Some answered Latin, Hebrew or Jewish, and then away we went.

One time the class accused me of always exaggerating or stretching things. I told them about the stylistic argument ploy of *reductio ad absurdum*. It reveals a process of refutation on the ground absurd and patently untenable consequences ensue from accepting an item at issue. My suggestion would be so outlandish it required rejection.

This gave me an opening to tell one of my favorite stories. Following a speaker's adage about putting myself into the story to lend a modicum of believability, I told them when younger I exaggerated a lot. The most notorious incident came when I rushed into my home shouting, "There's a bear in the yard, there's a bear in the yard." The first time, my mother came running out to protect her young from the bear, only to find no such animal in the yard.

The next time I came running in shouting, "The bear is in the yard, he's back in the yard," my mother reacted, but not as I expected. She led me into the closet in my room, instructed me to talk to God about telling the truth, and shut the door.

I waited an appropriate time before venturing out.

"Well, did you talk to God about telling the truth about a bear in our yard?"

"Yes, I did," I meekly answered.

"What did God say?"

"Really, you want to know what God said?"

"Yes, please," she insisted.

"God told me, the first time she saw that dog, she thought it was a bear too."

The class laughed and looked at me with a slight hint of incredulity.

One sixteen-year-old girl in class proved particularly hard to engage despite my verbal tricks. When I questioned her, she spoke softly, but used short answers. Her reticence puzzled me and made me think something else went on in her head. Polite to a fault, she caused no stir, but appeared distant from the class. She made no effort to disrupt the class. She sat quietly; therefore, I never offered the option of going somewhere else during class. After a few attempts to get her involved, I decided not to push her, to see if she developed more interest as the year went along. I continued to call on her but did not push it if she resisted.

Senior high youth trying to figure out who they are, get pressures from all around to behave one way or another. They struggle to learn how to live their lives. Tim Hiller, in his book *Strive: Life is Short, Pursue What Matters* writes, "External actions are evidence of internal beliefs. Our deeds are what show our creeds."

I firmly believe we learn from observing others, maybe more than hearing a teacher. I thought about applying this principle to our class. I hoped to instill in the teens how we live our lives shows who we *really* are, and this thought brought me to the social principles of the church. It occurred to me the social principles of the United Methodist Church might be a way to engage the youth because many teens gravitate to social issues and show passion toward them. Teens are keenly aware of the world around them and hold strong opinions on many social issues. This fact surprised me but allowed us to make progress in discussing how we want to live our lives.

Since its founding, the church took positions relating to social justice. Early Methodists strongly opposed slave trading, smuggling, and cruel treatment of prisoners. Over a hundred years ago, the church adopted a social creed and every four years at the General Conference of the United Methodist Church, the church body considers new principles relating to the modern world. The church's social principles are an attempt to convey a prayerful and thoughtful message about the human issues in our contemporary world based upon a biblical and theological foundation. The church offers the social principles as a prayerful and studied dialogue of faith and practice.

A preamble to the church's social principles in the early twenty-first century included the following: *"Grateful for God's forgiving love, in which we live and by which we are judged, and affirming our belief in the inestimable worth of each individual, we renew our commitment to become faithful witnesses to the gospel, not alone to the ends of the earth, but also to the depths of our common life and work."*

Our common life and work to me meant everything we do in our lives—how we live. Our class took this on as an educational process.

The church lays out social concerns for our natural world: air, water, soil, and plants. It extolls the virtue of examining our use of energy resources, animal life, and outer space. The principle affirms the validity of science in describing the natural world and recognizes technology as a legitimate use of God's natural world to enhance human life.

Additional social principles relate to our community, families, other Christian communities, marriage, divorce, single persons, gender equality, human sexuality, violence, abuse, sexual harassment, abortion, adoption, care of the dying, and suicide. This surprised most teens to learn the church examined these issues and took positions on them. The church also addressed property, collective bargaining, poverty, migrant workers, gambling, family farms, and corporate responsibility. The social principles address nearly all aspects of our lives, including basic freedoms, human rights, education, civil obedience, or disobedience, criminal and restorative justice, military service, and political policy.

The church attempts to live out these principles in how it operates. Investing church endowments and retirement funds includes these social principles. The social principles require avoiding investments in companies producing alcohol, tobacco, pornography, and nuclear arms. The church also uses shareholder activism to urge the pursuit of policies and products comporting with the social principles.

When the George W. Bush administration urged the United States to pursue military action in Iraq during 2002, the United Methodist Church spoke out against it. This stance introduced me and our class to the Doctrine of Just War as spelled out by the church. The basis for a "just war" revolves around a "just cause" where a decision for war is made as a response to a serious evil, such as an attack. The doctrine includes a "just intent" where the ends sought include the restoration of peace and justice, not total devastation of another nation. A last resort tradition lays out a presumption against going to war until every possibility of a peaceful settlement fails. Finally, the doctrine dictates a reasonable hope of success—subjecting one's people to suffering and sacrifice for a suicidal conflict cannot be justified.

In October 2002, Bishop Sharon A. Brown Christopher, president of the United Methodist Council of Bishops, penned a pastoral letter to all United Methodists. It addressed the Iraq war promoted by President Bush. She stated a pre-emptive war by the U.S. against Iraq goes against the grain of our understanding of the Gospel, our church's teaching, and our conscience.

Hope United Methodist Church serves a relatively affluent congregation in a wealthy suburb of Denver, Colorado. As such, the typical mix of political parties and socially progressive or conservative members belong to the congregation. Most teens expressed surprise the church took a stand. They thought the church avoided politics. The church's stand pleased some in the congregation, angered others. For the most part, the teens seemed pleased the church took stands on such issues.

We used the social principles of the church for class discussions. They gave a good platform for acknowledging class members and encouraging them to examine their beliefs. We enjoyed wide-ranging discussions and got most of the class involved. I enjoyed the give and take and settled into a comfortable role as teacher/leader of the class. Using some of my legal skills added to my comfort level.

Some social issues continued to roil the United Methodist Church after I retired from teaching. Homosexuality, transgender, and same sex marriage issues remain contentious issues for the Church. Ordination of Elders in the United Methodist Church remains forbidden to self-avowed homosexuals. These issues came home to the Rocky Mountain Conference of the United Methodist Church in 2016, when a gay woman, married to another woman, became Bishop of the Conference. The issue remained unresolved in mid-2018.

Despite recognizing the knowledge of and opinions on social issues held by teens, before long, I realized many in the class lacked a basic understanding of the Christian faith. Having a robust discussion about the church's positions on social principles showed progress, but I thought we needed more. I began to think of other topics and areas for study. What could we do to help build their faith? Some ideas popped into my mind.

I also concluded I might enjoy leading the class for more than a year or two. If so, I thought more about having some structure to the curriculum. Obviously, a fourteen-year-old freshman would spend only four years in class before becoming an eighteen-year-old senior. Rarely did a class member attend the class for more than four years.

Recognizing this, my lazy tendencies kicked in. A rotating list of four topics? Each taking a yearlong study? Then every fifth year we repeat an earlier topic. This way, whichever topic came around, it would be new to the incoming freshmen.

To address the basics of Christianity, I looked at a one-year study plan for a survey of the New Testament. We included the Gospels, Acts of the Apostles, Paul's letters to the early churches, the pastoral letters and the big ending, Revelation, a topic for the ages and one to catch a lot of interest. The topic gave many building blocks for Christian basics, covered a wide territory, and easily lasted a year. It also generated lots of questions and study by the class.

Because Saint Paul wrote so much of the New Testament and gets credit for early Christian theology, his life and times made another topic for yearlong discussions. I called it "Heroes and Sheroes." This came before the controversy about using language to separate men from women and before our culture took gender inequality as seriously as today. I used this as a play on words clarifying women could be heroes too. It also reflected my thoughts of Paul as an early hero. Paul's life and writings led us to some interesting classes.

Other topics varied over the years, one dealing with grief born from the Columbine High School murders, another on the deaths of classmates. Such events created despair, doubts, and anxiety among the class and became catalysts for new and varied discussions in class.

Over several years, I decided to use a couple more yearlong topics. One dealt with Images of God. This topic dealt with how our perception of God leads us toward different assumptions about a living God in our lives. One image, God as a judge, came easily to me because of my father. This yearlong topic covered myriad images of God and the ramifications of those images.

The last of the four-year rotation became what I called Who Am I, Where Am I Going, What Tools Will I Take with Me, and What Will I Do When Something Goes Wrong? This stemmed from earlier yearlong topics of building a community of faith and ways your faith can help deal with anxiety. This topic evolved from difficult experiences of the class members and gave us great discussion points related to how we differ and yet, how much we are the same.

I noted my failure to reach that sixteen-year-old girl and get her engaged with the class and her church. Toward the end of the year, she stopped coming altogether. I hardly knew her parents, but soon learned they too dropped away from the church. I lost track. The girl and I ran into each other a year later. She had a year-old baby with her in the order line for the local sandwich shop. She looked away when she saw me, but I walked up and spoke to her. I commented on her cute baby and mentioned I enjoyed seeing her. She told me she lived with an aunt while trying to finish her GED and, although her baby filled her with joy, her life was tough.

We chatted the few minutes while we ordered sandwiches. She offered tidbits of her life—she worked at a department store, her pregnancy embarrassed her parents, they divorced over differences in how to deal with her and the baby, how her aunt became a life-saver, and she did not stay in touch with any of the teens at the church. Soon time came to part. I offered some lame sounding platitudes—wish you well, hope things turn out for you, sorry for your troubles. Not knowing what else to say, I blurted out, "I love you." I then thought, why didn't I think of this first? She looked down at the floor, then at the baby, and then at me. "Thanks." She turned to leave.

Efforts to acknowledge teens, encourage them, and to love them do not always turn out the way we want. Could I shown more support to this young lady? What could I learn from this experience? Those questions remain with me.

Another teen under construction. My failure as much as hers.

CHAPTER FIVE

The 7-Eleven Trial

One issue looms large in the social principles: the death penalty. The issue attracts the public's attention every time a heinous crime occurs and the prosecutors ask for the death penalty. One such occurrence stemmed from the Aurora theater shooting in July 2012 when twelve persons died and seventy others suffered gunshot wounds. After a long trial, the jury found the defendant guilty, but declined to impose the death penalty.

Trial and appeal costs before an execution occurs cause some to argue in favor of abolishing the death penalty on a strictly economic basis. Others object on moral or humanitarian grounds. In Colorado, a majority of citizens continue to support the death penalty. The last Colorado execution occurred in 1997 and prompted much public discussion of the issue. Why not bring the issue to the teens of Hope UMC?

Knowing several attorneys from my days practicing law allowed me to ask for opinions and suggestions on the topic. I knew lawyers who worked as prosecutors for district attorneys and I knew criminal defense lawyers. All suggested, for a group of teenagers, success included making the discussion realistic or personal. They told me death penalty cases amplify the emotional factor for those involved by ten. If we could create personal involvement, get the teens focused, a successful exercise or debate would follow. This gave me an idea.

The class knew I once practiced law, but did not know much about my work history. What if I concocted a story, involving a murder trial and me as one of the lawyers involved? Could it seem realistic for the class? Even better, what if I could tell the story from my personal point of view as a participant and let someone play the role of the defendant. Seeing me present the case as protagonist, and seeing the defendant or villain tell another side of the story, might create some reality for the class.

One of my best friends for many years could play the villain perfectly. Some years back I asked him, when I faced a separation and pending divorce, if I could stay at his house and couch surf for a while. He said, "Sure, come on over." I stayed for three years. He is what I call a good friend.

A lawyer, a bit eccentric, he loved a good tale. Convince him to help me, my next step. I laid out the project and asked if he knew anyone to play the villain.

Being smarter than me, or maybe because he knew me well, he did not take the bait when we first discussed the idea. Too proud to tell him right then I wanted him to do it, I waited a few days before approaching him again and admitting I wanted him to play the role. Would he do it? He agreed on one condition: I let him write the script for the defendant/villain. Of course, I agreed.

We intended to have some fun, bring the legal process/ death penalty issue to life, and give the youth at church an opportunity to think about and discuss the issue. The basics went like this: Colorado law provided for the death penalty, protection of individual rights came by allowing legal representation, trial, and appeals. Underlying themes included punishment/revenge, the death penalty as deterrent, the morality of taking one's life in the pursuit of justice, and taxpayer costs resulting from the process.

We planned to tell our tale in front of the youth group on a Sunday evening late in the fall. I pretended I once served as an assistant district attorney and prosecuted a murder trial, seeking the death penalty for a man named Mike Centro. I suggested I strongly supported the idea of justice for victims and proper punishment, including the death penalty, for those found guilty.

We dreamed up a factual basis for the case. A twenty-four-year-old female, while working as a clerk at a 7-Eleven store, died of gunshot wounds received during a robbery. The robbery occurred at approximately 2:00 a.m. Before dying, she gave paramedics a description of a man: mid-thirties, dark brown hair, mustache, 5 foot 10 inches, 135 pounds and of slight build. Two other witnesses in town gave similar descriptions of a man who visited a bar in town, tried to buy cigarettes, and asked directions to Greeley on the same night of the robbery/murder.

One witness identified Mike Centro, saying he followed her car, pulled up to the bar and followed her inside. This lady said it upset her and she told the bartender when the man appeared. The bartender took down the license number of the car the man drove. Both the woman and the bartender clearly saw the man in the bar, and because of the unusual circumstances, remembered his face. After he learned the bar sold no cigarettes, the man received directions to the nearest 7-Eleven store.

Police found the murder weapon about a mile from the store, but no fingerprints.

The defendant on two previous occasions dealt in stolen auto parts. The authorities dropped both earlier cases on technicalities.

The license number traced to his auto and the police arrested him. A search warrant produced a rag with the same type of oil as found on the murder weapon. He admitted trying to buy cigarettes at the bar, getting directions to the 7-Eleven, and going there and seeing the attendant. He denied everything else and insisted he left without incident.

The bartender went to the 7-Eleven soon after closing the bar and found the attendant lying behind the counter, shot. The 911 call came in at 2:24 a.m. On the way to the hospital, the clerk gave a description of the man who shot her. She died right after reaching the hospital.

Direct evidence at the trial put the defendant at the scene within minutes of the crime. As part of the prosecution, I showed two positive identifications of the defendant at the bar, his admission of being at the 7-Eleven, and the oily rag from his car. The prosecution showed no direct link to the murder weapon, but I felt the weight of the evidence pointed to the defendant.

The defendant refused to plea bargain despite the threat of the death penalty. He adamantly claimed his innocence. A jury found him guilty and imposed a death sentence.

I planned to unveil the rest of the story before the teens as their young minds absorbed the impact of the death penalty, even for what shaped up as a cold-blooded murder. The backstory for Mr. Centro followed. Mike Centro held a job at an automotive service center as a mechanic, lived in an apartment, liked to hunt and fish, owned firearms, and never earned much money. He lost his previous job due to suspicions of selling stolen auto parts. He claimed the prosecution slanted the evidence against him.

His story: hard worker, honest, and a victim of circumstances. He only tried to help someone. He talked to the lady and the bartender, wanted some cigarettes, went to the 7-Eleven by following their directions, bought some cigarettes, and went home. He insisted he could not kill anyone and the charges did not fit him. He would not plea bargain for something he did not do.

By the time the trial came up, feeling angry, and fearing a system stacked against him, he found himself in a helpless situation. No one but he and his family believed his story. He did not like the deputy district attorney (me), because I pushed for the conviction. He trusted the truth to come out at trial, but soon realized his mistake. It became clear to him his death would come from a jury failing to do the right thing.

After eighteen months in jail, fifteen on death row, while an appeal progressed, a Wyoming man confessed to the murder in the 7-Eleven. Investigators found proof of purchase for the murder weapon. He apparently decided to rob the 7-Eleven because he wanted money. When the attendant resisted, he shot her and hurriedly left the scene and fled to Wyoming. Later, a

Wyoming court found him guilty of another murder and his conscience led him to confess to the Colorado crime.

You can see the dilemma. The confession by the Wyoming man ultimately saved Mr. Centro, but what if the man remained silent? The state of Colorado and I could have caused an innocent man's death. Did a death penalty for Mr. Centro serve the public interest? Is there a Christian attitude toward capital punishment? We set the table, now we needed to serve the meal.

I appeared before the group to tell the tale. A large turnout showed up because word got around about having a guest speaker, a man convicted of a murder. My teenage sons came to see the show. I swore them to secrecy, because they knew Mr. Centro, as my good friend.

The room full of teens remained quiet. I spoke softly and solemnly. My personal involvement pulled in the group. The numerous details added to the realistic nature of the story. The alleged facts set up the quandary. Then, Mr. Centro addressed the group. I prefaced his introduction by saying they should treat him with the greatest courtesy because he suffered a great deal from the trial and his incarceration. His anger at me stemmed from me pursuing the case against him. I asked the class to listen to him, think about his story, and we would hold a discussion after Mr. Centro left.

My friend played the part with flair. No haircut for several weeks, a scraggly mustache, blue jean jacket with collar turned up, and a dark brown cowboy hat gave him the appearance of someone unaccustomed to appearing in a Methodist church. To top off this blue-collar appearance, he wore dark, wraparound sunglasses hiding his eyes from the audience. His delivery clearly displayed a chip on his shoulder and he expressed no love lost for me. He looked and acted like an angry person with a grudge against the world. He captivated the group.

Mr. Centro told the gathering he watched through the windows as I discussed the case with them and knew some of them thought capital punishment worked. He would tell his side of the issue.

"The justice system favors rich people like you," he told them plainly. "There are all kinds of obstacles for poor people and I don't know how someone who calls themselves Christian could support the death penalty. You call yourself a Christian, but how does that fit with thou shall not kill?"

He railed against those wanting prayer in schools and those who put their hand on the Bible to swear "so help me God" when testifying, but quickly said yes to putting someone to death. He called it hypocrisy, plain and simple.

"Capital punishment is okay so long as it is done to outcasts or those different from you. So long as it happens to black or brown people, you are okay with it. Most of you Christians avoid the moral aspect of capital punishment."

Everyone there felt his hot as fire anger. The performance captivated the teens. The group remained quiet and paused a long time when he asked for comments. Some finally spoke up. One asked about the process of disqualifying people from sitting on a jury if they opposed the death penalty. To Mr. Centro the system allowed this and he did not think it fair.

Another asked why he came to speak and how he felt about his entire experience.

"I came to see how a Christian group would treat me and hoped I might change someone's mind about capital punishment. A mistake almost cost me my life and too many of you are okay with it."

As Mr. Centro left the building, the group watched him through the windows along the south side of the fellowship hall. They were hushed until he reached the parking lot and his car. Then they all started talking at once, raising their voices to gain attention. The youth director and I assured everyone they would get time to talk, but we needed to proceed in an orderly fashion.

One teen indicated she felt no one held the right to play God and decide who lives and who dies. Some disagreed, but she held her ground saying she saw no moral cause for the death penalty. She felt even one death in error could not be tolerated. Her comments triggered others dealing with certainty, if they knew for sure, then they could support the death penalty. I told them Mr. Centro's circumstances, as we now understood, dealt with the certainty issue. Once I was certain he committed the murder, but later found out he did not. Absolute certainty would be nice, but it is a rare commodity in many cases.

Others said terrible crimes deserved the death penalty but could not adequately respond to the question of executing an innocent person by mistake. Others resignedly indicated they could go along with it because our laws included the death penalty. Still others wanted to take action, join a protest, or support those opposing the death penalty. The discussion went around and around with most everyone taking a turn expressing their thoughts.

One teen mentioned a similar discussion at school. The teacher asked for a show of hands and only three out of twenty-five students favored abolishing the death penalty in Colorado.

The teen told the group how the class verbally bullied and threatened those three who opposed capital punishment. The rest of the class called them clueless, easy on criminals, and naïve. Regardless, he held fast to his viewpoint and continued unconvinced. The group from Hope expressed support for him speaking his mind and condemned any bullying, even if they disagreed with his position.

I asked if they learned anything from the exercise. All agreed they did. What about anyone changing his or her view of capital punishment after meeting Mr. Centro? Only a couple of hands went up. I felt like the issue produced a good discussion, and got some teens thinking on a deeper level.

I must add a tragic note as dénouement to this story. Twenty-seven years after my friend appeared as Mike Centro before the youth of Hope, he attacked his wife with a hatchet, striking her about the head and shoulders multiple times and stabbed her repeatedly with a knife. He called 911 to report he murdered his wife. She, luckily, survived the ordeal.

Nearly two years later at the age of seventy, my friend pled guilty to attempted murder and received a sentence of twenty years in the Colorado penitentiary. The current law requires serving three-fourths of the sentence before becoming eligible for parole. This presents the probability he will die in prison. His current circumstances pain me deeply, but I remember fondly our friendship and his willingness to help promote a debate among teens. Unfortunately, later in life, he found his way to the under-construction list.

The young woman who spoke up to say no one should play God and decide if someone lives or dies? She became an award-winning teacher loved by students and colleagues alike. The A list definitely includes her.

CHAPTER SIX

For Unto Us a Child is Born

Christmastime cannot get any better for millions of young people around the world. Kids eagerly look forward to the day, make lists of gifts wanted, and often ask parents, "How many days before Christmas?"

The roots of gift giving and receiving associated with the commercial aspects of the season go deep in our culture, but Christians love Christmas because they reflect on the greatest gift ever—a Savior bringing forgiveness and eternal life.

I do not fret about the use of Xmas or getting Christ back into Christmas. For the youth of Hope church, my family, and me, Christ always belonged in the season. Because many families traveled or enjoyed the ski slopes of Colorado during Christmas week, our class began talking Christmas the first week of December. Regardless of our study for the year, we paused to reflect on Christmas.

Christmas Eve services often brought college-age youth back to Hope. I loved seeing them and catching up on their lives. We hugged and shared stories of our current activities. I mostly asked about their college experience, classes, and their love lives. I also wanted to know what they learned since graduating high school and it gave me a chance to hassle them one more time.

I greeted one particularly bright and inquiring former class member one Christmas Eve with a challenging lead. "I have been thinking about the whole space-time continuum and wondered if you learned anything at college about it. Do you think the universe will continue to expand infinitely, or at some point will it reach a boundary, and begin collapsing into itself so the whole process might be repeated?"

"It's interesting, Charlie. The same thing occurred to me." He grinned as if he really did think along those lines. "But, you probably know the new thinking is about parallel universes or multiverses. That's where the action is today."

I gave him a hug and told him to join his family because he obviously learned to take my jabs and return them with vigor.

Sometimes former students would attend the senior high class on a Sunday near Christmas and I always invited them to talk. Sometimes the visit involved their faith and other times what they remembered about the class when they attended. The guys talked about sports and how hard their classes became once they entered college. The women often talked about drama in the dorms and how some of the women in college showed more interest in a "Mrs." Degree than any other degree. Many regaled the class with "Charlie stories" and recounted some antic I exhibited when they were in the class. The current students ate it up.

Following my father's example where he annually read the Christmas story from Luke's gospel, I read the account for the class. Our talk covered the usual subjects. We mentioned angels, the shepherds, and no room at the inn. And, of course, how a baby came as perhaps the most ironic gift of all.

One Sunday in early December, I got to work with my love of, and wonder at, the stars of the heavens. We used the time to talk stars, especially the Star of Bethlehem. I asked who knew about a conjunction of planets or stars. On some occasions, a youth jumped in and let us know the facts about conjunctions. At other times, I led the discussion.

Many knew the classic definition of a conjunction, having seen Sesame Street's *Grammar Rock* during their childhood. "Conjunction junction, what's your function" rang out in the classroom. We reviewed a conjunction as a combination or association, a simultaneous occurrence of two conditions, and a word that connects other words in a sentence.

But, what about a planetary conjunction? This involves alignment of two or more planets, when seen from earth, appearing close together or as one.

"After Jesus was born in Bethlehem in Judea, during the time of King Herod, Magi from the east came to Jerusalem and asked: 'Where is the one who has been born King of the Jews? We saw his star in the east and came to worship him.' ...after they had heard the King, they went on their way, and the star they had seen in the east went ahead of them until it stopped over the place where the child was. When they saw the star, they were overjoyed." Matthew 2:1-2, 9-10.

No record exists of the exact year of Jesus' birth. From the historical record, we know it came between 12 BCE and 7 CE.

For centuries, astronomers observed and recorded the planets and stars. They predicted certain events and recorded others. Today's computers run reverse progressions of planetary orbits to show where planets appeared in their orbits at various times in the past.

During the period for Jesus' birth, the data show two planetary conjunctions. In 7 CE Jupiter and Saturn appeared close to each other when observed from earth, close enough they looked like one star. These two biggest planets in our solar system can appear quite bright in the sky, the conjunction created an extremely bright, heavenly light.

Another conjunction occurred in 2 BCE. This conjunction involved Jupiter and Venus. Jupiter as the biggest planet and Venus as one of the closest to the sun, shine brighter than other planets. These two in close proximity to each other in a viewer's line of sight made an exceedingly bright light in the sky. Jupiter and Venus are approximately 400 million miles apart, but from earth, they can appear close to each other depending on where they reside in their orbits. I thought demonstrating this would be fun and get us out of the classroom at the same time.

For this we moved to the Fellowship Hall, a large room used for meals, classes, or functions. Other than a few folks drinking coffee, the room remained empty during our class hours. We took the class there and used a couple of volunteers for Jupiter and Venus. While the rest of us assembled in the middle of the room, I placed the Venus volunteer close to us and indicated an orbit only a short distance from the main group. I told Venus to walk fast around the orbit. Jupiter took its place much farther from the main group and walked slowly around its orbit. When the two came close to each other in the main group's line of sight, I yelled, "Stop!"

The planet volunteers paused in their orbits and the class could see, from our point of view, how they appeared close to each other. We talked about vast distances involved and how such a conjunction could be mistaken for one star. All decorum deteriorated when others joined the Venus and Jupiter volunteers and began racing around their orbits.

I doubt many remember the astronomy lesson, but I trust they remember one of the Christmas symbols—the Star of Bethlehem.

During following Sundays in December, we used the time to discuss other symbols of Christmas. I asked the class for suggestions. We got "the mall," "toy commercials," "those red buckets the Salvation Army uses," "brightly wrapped packages," and "Christmas trees." I congratulated them, but indicated Christmas includes even more symbols.

"How about lights?" I asked. We use Christmas lights on our houses and trees to remind us the Christ child came as the light of the world. A discussion quickly ensued about whose home or neighborhood contained houses with the most Christmas lights. Some reported extravagant displays at their homes, so special they appeared on local television stations.

"We mentioned Christmas trees," I continued. A popular legend holds Martin Luther cut down the first Christmas tree and decorated it with candles to symbolize the stars in the Bethlehem sky on the night of Jesus' birth. Likewise, we use evergreen trees to remind us Christ is present in our lives.

"What about snowflakes?" On we went although few seemed to know snowflakes as symbols of Christmas. I asked them to think about our lives as snowflakes. Both consist mainly of water and last for a limited time. They knew each snowflake, like people, is unique. Nearly six billion of us on the planet and no two alike.

"Who thinks of a candy cane as a symbol of Christmas?" Only a few raised a hand. I mentioned the legend about the candy maker who wanted to invent a candy to represent his Christian faith. He used hard candy because he thought of Christ as the Rock of Ages. He shaped the candy into the curve of the shepherd's staff. Also, to remind us how the shepherd always looks for the lost sheep. The basic white color to the candy reminded him of Christ's purity and the red stripe stood for the blood of Christ shed for others. The three thinner red stripes reminded him of the stripes Jesus received when the Roman soldiers whipped him. Sometimes the candy cane includes a green stripe the maker used to remind us Jesus came as a gift for all. In addition, the peppermint flavor reminded the candy maker of hyssop, a herb from the mint family, used in the Hebrew Bible for purification and sacrifice. Supposedly, this reminded the candy maker of Jesus' sacrifice for the sins of the world.

"Who knew so much about candy canes?" One almost bewildered class member blurted out.

"And what about the nativity scene?" I said. We attribute the origin of the crèche or nativity scene to St. Francis of Assisi. During his life, most people could not read and did not know the story of Jesus' birth. Many treated Christmas as any other day. St. Francis set up a stable near the village filled with animals, hay, and a manger. He recruited a couple to play Mary and Joseph and asked them to bring their own baby along for the tableau. His foresight gave the villagers a picture of the Christmas story

Author, in top hat, with group for Holiday Dinner

to see and understand. Many homes today, including those of many in our class, include such scenes during the Christmas season.

When we gathered as a family during my youth, my mother always encouraged the youngest kids to create a skit and portray the Christmas story. Our family of six children, eighteen grandchildren, and at times, a neighbor kid or two, accommodated the main characters, Mary & Joseph, but also kings, shepherds, and the innkeeper. Everyone got a part. A slightly used doll typically became the baby Jesus. The adults overlooked the occasional missing limb or errant eye of the baby Jesus. This made great theater.

One Christmas a new grandchild blessed the family and a real baby joined the cast. The characters went through their parts with great solemnity and seriousness. When the kings and shepherds gathered around the baby Jesus, Mary, played by an inspired six-year-old, blurted out, "Our Jesus is ALIVE!" Moreover, for Christians, this is true throughout the year.

Then, on the Sunday before Christmas, I asked the class several questions to stimulate discussion. They included, tell me about some of the gifts you've received for Christmas. Can you remember your favorite gift of all time? And, the favorite gift you gave someone at Christmas? I ended by asking if anyone ever received gold, frankincense, or myrrh. Some reported gold jewelry, but no frankincense or myrrh.

We also discussed family traditions around Christmas. I asked who exchanged gifts on Christmas Eve and who waited until Christmas morning. Most waited until Christmas morning, but many said their parents let them open one gift on Christmas Eve. I told them my family followed this method with the wrinkle being my mother selected the gift. Many confirmed the same pattern at their homes and quickly reported mothers' choices invariably brought pajamas, underwear, socks, or some other unexciting gift.

This must be a universal trait; practical mothers know how to build suspense and anticipation.

CHAPTER SEVEN

Secret to a Happy Life

Our life's experiences come along any time we interact with others. I decided to use an example as a teaching tool. I called it "The Secret to a Happy Life" and tried to use the story as a stand-alone lesson once a year, regardless of our annual topic.

Keeping your life in balance is the goal. I drew a circle on the board and divided it into three equal sections. I labeled the sections physical, intellectual, and spiritual. Then we talked about common activities in each of these realms of our existence. I wrote them out on the pertinent section of the circle. *Physical*—eating, sleeping, exercise, and so on; *Intellectual*—reading, study, preparing papers, etc.; and *Spiritual*—praying, attending church, and spending time with a community of faith.

Then I told the class a story about a young man and a young woman. I began, "Long, long, ago in a galaxy far, far, away." The well-known catch phrase got their attention. All teens know the Star Wars introduction and because some were rolling their eyes, I knew they must wonder how Charlie could use it in a Sunday school class. At least, they showed interest.

I continued the story. Once a teenage couple thoroughly enjoyed their world. They dated steadily for several years. When they were in the first grade, they took part in a make-believe wedding in a children's play called *The Wedding of the Flowers.* Everyone got a part, but this boy and girl received speaking parts. In the play they married and lived happily ever after in a wonderful garden full of flowers. Most participants played daisies or roses along with dancing and singing. The pastor officiating the wedding played a Jack in the Pulpit flower, the bride, a Chrysanthemum and the groom, a Carnation. The speaking parts for bride and groom? Each said, "I do."

They belonged to the same church, were both good students active in many activities, and were often together from first grade forward. Popular in high school, they enjoyed their lives and no worries clouded their future.

In the fall of their junior year, each almost seventeen years old, an historic event shocked the world. The assassination of John F. Kennedy occurred in Dallas, Texas on November 22, 1963. About noon that day, the couple headed into the lunch-room at school when a voice on the public-address system announced someone shot President Kennedy. By early afternoon, they learned he died from the gunshot wounds.

Another event soon took place and shook their individual lives much more than Kennedy's assassination. At the movies on date night, while seated in the audience, the fellow put his right arm around the girl's shoulder and squeezed her gently.

She screamed out, startling him and everyone in the theater. Doing the same thing many times before never got such a response.

After several visits to the doctors, they learned of a calcium deposit embedded in her right shoulder. By early spring 1964, cancer specialists confirmed cancer in the tangled mass in her shoulder. Doctors recommended removing it.

The doctors cut a large mass from her shoulder, leaving a huge indentation about three inches in diameter. Obviously, no hugging the shoulder for some time, but they continued to date and enjoy each other's company. Both pretended everything remained fine. Before long, they learned the cancer returned. This time it spread, requiring more treatment.

The girl's parents knew of the Mayo Clinic in Minnesota and its sterling reputation. She went there for evaluation. Some of the top cancer specialists in the world confirmed the cancer spread across her shoulder and arm. They recommended amputation of her right arm. During the summer of 1964, the young girl, who happened to be right handed, lost her right arm to amputation. In fact, they cut away about a fourth of her including her shoulder blade/clavicle, bicep, deltoid, pectoralis major, elbow, forearm, and hand. Gone! She looked dramatically different and leaned a little to the right. Her blouses and shirts drooped where her shoulder and arm used to be. People looked away when she came into view, but she possessed a strong faith and struck a bold path ahead.

She learned to write left-handed. Being a majorette in the band required twirling a baton and leading the band during performances so she learned left-handed routines. Her friends supported and encouraged her. Her appearance with the band for the first football game her senior year produced an emotional night for all concerned. Maybe her troubles were over.

Of course, she and the boyfriend were scared, but because they lived blessed lives until then, their optimism continued. She handled the entire situation better than he did. His worldview of happily growing up, getting married to his school sweetheart, and having a family became fuzzy and uncertain. He knew many cancer patients survived only five years or less after diagnosis. She continued as an honor student and garnered scholarships for college. As a better-than-average athlete, he put most of his energy into sports and went to college with a basketball scholarship. They dated still, but he pulled back in many ways from a close emotional attachment.

About a year went by without incident and their lives adjusted to the stress of her illness. By early 1966, the stress increased. The cancer spread to her lung, necessitating another surgery to remove a lobe. Her weight dropped to ninety pounds and she lost all her hair from chemotherapy treatments. Often her nausea from chemo sidelined her for days at a time, but she continued in college, becoming an honor student. He felt for her and despaired how the treatments savaged her once healthy body. He also despaired because he could do nothing about it.

He became angry, with God, the Vietnam War, the world, almost everything, and decided to throw all his energy into something he could control—sports. They continued dating but did not talk much about the future any more.

His basketball career took the first two years of college and provided enjoyment and accolades. However, lacking the skills to play at a major level, he realized his dream of playing professional basketball made no sense. This forced a change in his emphasis. He switched his focus to studies, college, and then law school. He worked hard at being a student. He graduated college in four years, taking a full load each semester. Law schools in Colorado accepted him and he immediately enrolled after getting his under-graduate degree. His plan became to enter graduate school and hope his draft board would delay military service until he finished, but things turned out differently.

On Friday afternoon August 22, 1969, after finishing his final exam for the first semester in law school, he returned to his rented home to find his parent's car in the driveway. Seeing the car puzzled him because they lived five hundred miles away and he received no advance news of a visit. His parents informed him the girl died the day before of a massive brain hemorrhage, barely five years from discovering the cancer in her shoulder. They delayed telling him until he finished his law school exams.

Within two weeks of her death, he went into the armed forces, serving with the Marines. Fortunately, for him, he avoided Vietnam, and served stateside. His anger, confusion, and distance from God continued for several years.

The fellow did not regularly pray or attend worship services after this. After the military service, he put all his energy into finishing his law studies and passing the Bar Examination in Colorado. As a brand-new lawyer, he looked forward to his career and most of his energy went into his career and the practice of law. He married right before he turned twenty-two and loved the addition of two boys to his family, but the marriage failed. He and his wife were not well matched and the marriage suffered accordingly. Soon the marriage dissolved. He did not sleep well, became agitated at little things, and worried about his purpose in life. His stomach ached constantly.

Almost ten years after the girl's death, he drove past a United Methodist Church and decided to stop in. He talked with a staff member and learned of the worship service times. He attended the next Sunday, by himself, sitting at the back row, hoping no one would see him. He did, however, sign the attendance sheet, but used his business address instead of his home address thinking no one would call on him at this office.

The next Wednesday, an associate pastor came to the fellow's office unannounced, just to chat. Later he explained it as a Holy Spirit thing, something with no other explanation. The elderly pastor possessed a warm, friendly, welcoming way. After a five-minute conversation of this and that, and getting some history on one another, the pastor said, "You strike me as someone who wants to be part of something bigger than yourself. The church can provide this if you let it." He paused and did not say anything for a few seconds. "I hope to see you again," and stood to leave.

After a handshake and some final pleasantries, the pastor left. Afterwards the fellow contemplated the conversation and reflected on the visit. The pastor's easy-going, no-pressure style and dedication impressed him.

A few weeks passed before the fellow returned to the worship service, but he soon found himself welcomed and renewed. Several people made him part of the group. He felt good about this and remembered some of his happiest times came when he associated with a community of faith. Maybe the church held something for him. It finally dawned on this fellow; he spent a lot of time concentrating on one thing and neglecting others. During all his struggles, triumphs, and endeavors for the past ten years, the spiritual part of his life suffered neglect. His anger at God estranged him from any type of spiritual development, participation, or discernment. Could this be a link to his unhappiness?

I told the class, the fellow in the story decided to keep his life in balance. Not to stress only one part of his life, but to pay attention and invest time and effort into all parts of his existence. He worked at physical matters—exercise, eating better, taking care of his body. He also worked at the intellectual side—reading outside of work, joining a public speaking club, taking classes on interesting subjects. Finally, he returned to investing in his spiritual side, working to reacquaint himself with the church, his faith, and a robust community of faith.

The lesson learned became keep the different spheres of your life in balance, don't concentrate on one part of your life to the detriment of others. Remember the spiritual side of our lives matters. Put effort into all three areas and you become a happier person, no matter what happens in your life. Of course, I finally told the class the truth. I lived this story. I too, spent several years on the under-construction list.

One never knows if teens are listening or getting the gist of what you present, but this lesson proved effective, at least for a couple of the class members. Years later, I got a heart-felt letter from a young woman who related an unhappy time at college. She attended college on a volleyball scholarship but struggled with her studies and her personal life. She told me as she struggled; she recalled this lesson from church. She called it "putting all your eggs in one basket." She applied the principle of the lesson to her life and things began turning around. She flattered me by saying I stood for an affirming and empowering influence for her. She wanted me to know I, and this lesson, made a huge difference in her life. She thanked me for sharing this story from my life.

Another Sunday a young man returned to church from his college studies and said he wanted to show me something. Glad to see him, I said nothing about my puzzlement at his comment. I wondered what he wanted to show me. What could not be shown right there in the church foyer? After the usual greetings following the worship service, we met in the youth room. He pulled up his long-sleeved shirt to reveal a tattoo on his bicep, a three-pointed Celtic Knot. He said it reflected his Irish heritage, part of what we discussed in the "Who Am I" year of study. More importantly to him, the tattoo reminded him to seek balance in his life. That particular lesson influenced him and he wanted to remember it. Later, this young man asked me to assist in his wedding ceremony by reading Scriptures.

Celtic Knot tattoo as reminder to stay balanced

These two people appear on the accomplished list and remembering them warms my heart.

CHAPER EIGHT

Wit and Wisdom of Teenagers

Looking for a topic to introduce the class to the basics of the Christian faith and not bore them to death, I started with the foundation—the Bible. The idea seemed simple enough, but when you think about it, not so much. Some teens knew the Bible, but many only knew it as this powerful book, a perennial best seller, and a book many quoted, or in my judgment, often misquoted.

How do you cover the Bible, its contents, its truths, and its wisdom, in an hour on Sunday mornings nine months of the year? Difficult, to say the least. I decided beginning at the beginning, Genesis, made sense. Everyone, surely, knew the creation story. Did they know Genesis contains two creation stories? How were the two stories alike and how did they differ? Should we take the words literally? Were Adam and Eve actual, real, living human beings? Many questions come from the first book in the Bible.

Teenagers often hold opinions, they may not be informed opinions, but they have them nonetheless. I wanted to see what they thought and sought to make the endeavor fun. What if we took the story and class members played the roles of the people in the stories? Wanting to keep interest and to be gender neutral, I thought about doing the roles with Adam, and then Eve created from one of his ribs, in the traditional pattern. But, what if we reverse the story? Eve, then Adam from her rib?

We played both the pattern most of them recognized: Adam wakes up and finds Eve, then take the story from there, but also play it with reversed the roles. The boys and girls reacted differently, and I found their imagined dialogue quite interesting.

I let the girls go first. When we reversed the story and Eve awakens to find Adam, some of the girls took the opportunity to reset gender equality. We saw women's liberation in action. Some examples from Eve waking to find Adam: "Go fix us a meal. Then, clean up this place, and be quiet because I want to sleep." "What are you doing here? I do not need any help. I can do everything by myself." "I see you are late. Where have you been? I have been waiting for some time now."

The girls loved it, but the boys, not so much. Even a hint of role reversal or masculine inferiority made them anxious. Not one of the males articulated his fears, but you could almost see the wheels turning in their minds. At least the exercise made everyone pause and reflect on the story. In Genesis, the man comes first in the story, but what if the culture of the time turned female-centric? When their turn came, most boys looked to assert the typical male attitudes, partly because they believed them and partly in reaction to the girls' take on a whimsical first conversation. Some went like this: "I need a sandwich. And, get me a soda while you're up." "Hurry up; we don't want to be late. How long does it take to fix your hair?" "I am the boss; you need to do what I say."

Most of the boys liked this approach, but the ladies hooted and hollered.

One sensitive and mature fellow, Bryce Harman, took a completely different turn. When given Adam's role, where he awakens and finds Eve, and then improvises the conversation, he paused, dramatically rubbed his eyes as if in disbelief, and then said, "Whoa! Man! This is going to be fun." The class hesitated, but I immediately understood his play on words—woman—so I burst out laughing. After a few seconds, when the class caught on, everyone joined in the laughter.

The Old Testament can be daunting and I found it that way, but our search for lessons to convey wisdom and hold interest continued. Next, we looked at Proverbs and added a twist for teens.

I couched the Proverbs as iterations of what King Soloman learned. I hoped the class would come up with some things they learned.

Some of the class knew Proverbs as King Solomon's collection of moral and religious maxims, but most could not define the word. We discussed pithy sayings that draw sharp contrast between wisdom and folly or righteousness and sin.

Later, we went through the book of Proverbs, noting its prologue, structure, and general topics. Many were surprised to learn the book covered many topics; love, faithfulness, trust in God, wisdom, joy, honesty, pride, quarrels, and quick tempers.

We also tied some proverbs to the social principles of the Church. A couple of examples:

"If a man shuts his ears to the cry of the poor, he too will cry out and not be answered." Proverbs 21:13

"Speak up for those who cannot speak for themselves, for the rights of all who are destitute. Speak up and judge fairly; defend the rights of the poor and needy. Proverbs 31:8-9

My favorite proverb and my view relating directly to teenagers: "*Train a child in the way he should go, and when he is old, he will not depart from it." Proverbs 22:6.* I stress to parents of teens the proverb says "when he is *old,* he will not depart from it" not when he is a teenager and filled with rebellion. Don't we all seek this? Training children in the ways they should go, with honesty, character, and intelligence. I believe God must be patient with all of us, especially, teenagers, because at some point we all find ourselves under construction.

We discussed many selected proverbs at length, including the following:

"The fear of the Lord is the beginning of knowledge, but fools despise wisdom and discipline." 1:7

"Trust in the Lord with all your heart and lean not on your own understanding; in all your ways acknowledge him, and he will make your paths straight." 3:5

The kids quickly homed in on these two and mentioned they came to church wanting to understand God better. They also acknowledged knowing some fools who lacked discipline.

"Go to the ant, you sluggard; consider its ways and be wise! It has no commander, no overseer or ruler, yet it stores its provisions in summer and gathers its food at harvest." 6:6

Some teens acknowledged their parents or grandparents called them lazy at one time or another. Others mentioned never thinking about an ant having a commander or boss and felt they could learn from this one.

"A gentle answer turns away wrath, but a harsh word stirs up anger." 15:1

"Better a meal of vegetables where there is love than a fatted calf with hatred." 15:17

"Even a fool is thought wise if he keeps silent, and discerning if he holds his tongue." 17:28

"He who answers before listening–that is his folly and shame." 18:13

Several classes identified with these. One teen said he thought Abe Lincoln said something similar about holding your tongue, remaining silent and people will think you are smart, open your mouth too much and you remove all doubts.

We spent a month working through the book of Proverbs. The timeliness of many sayings and the application to modern times impressed the class. They saw parallels in their lives with anger, wisdom, and industriousness. Some mentioned how teens can quickly gossip and human foibles remain constant for ages. Some thought they should be on bumper stickers or perhaps reflected by an emoji on their smart phones.

The last week of this study, I told the class to create their own proverbs. I collected many of them for my files.

The instructions were, "Pretend you are King Solomon and you want your experience and wisdom to pass down to future generations. What would you say? Write your own proverbs using the format: I've learned . . . and then complete the sentence."

Here are some of my favorites—out of the minds of teenagers—some wisdom for the ages:

I've learned you have to go get an education; an education won't come and get you. Age 16.

I've learned God loves you, no matter what. Age 15.

I've learned a bad sport is selfish. Age 17.

I've learned there is more to life than my SAT score. Age 17.

I've learned if you want to make friends, you have to go to others first. Age 14.

I've learned you have to trust God, no matter what. Age 18.

I've learned you can't make everyone happy. Age 16.

I've learned you are never fully dressed without a smile. Age 16.

I've learned with God, you are never alone. Age 17.

I've learned people who tell you how nice they are probably aren't. Age 15.

I've learned you can have fun even though you don't follow the crowd. Age 17.

I've learned stress is often self-inflicted. Age 18.

I've learned you enjoy life more if you prove to your parents they can trust you. Age 18.

I've learned common sense is the least common of the senses. Age 16.

I've learned teenaged guys are immature, and easily amused. Age 15.

I've learned there is no time but the present. The past exists only in our memory and the future only in our imagination. Age 18.

I've learned jumping on a thin branch in a two-story tree is a bad idea. Age 14.

I've learned driving is not as easy as it appears, especially with a stick shift. Age 15.

I've learned bad things happen to good people. Age 16.

I've learned boys are like porta-pottys. They all smell bad and are full of poo, but sometimes you *really* need one. Age 17.

Before we finished, some of the witty, sarcastic, and clever among us, could not pass up the opportunity to razz the teacher or show their sense of humor. These are some of my favorites. To be taken with several grains of salt.

I've learned who I am, where I am going, what tools I will take with me, and what I will do when something goes wrong. Age 17. (This person deserves a spot on the A list for remembering this from our lessons.)

I've learned "um" should never start a sentence. Age 16. (Ditto for this person.)

I've learned not to mess with Charlie. Age 18.

I've learned Charlie knows lots of big words. Age 17.

I've learned Jesus is the right answer to everything. Age 16. This one grew out of a discussion where I asked a question no one could answer. One of the sharper teens said, "I think the answer is Jesus. Jesus is always a good answer." We all chuckled and for the next several sessions, when someone did not know the answer to a question, he would answer, "Jesus." I started giving credit for creativity, if not originality.

I've learned if, at first, you don't succeed, skydiving is not for you. Age 15.

I've learned ppl who spel wrds only 1 wy, hve no imagginotion." [Sic] Age 17. Sarcasm of the first order because when criticized for misspelling a word I wrote on the board, I quoted this statement from my maternal grandmother, Mary Ellen Gowdy, an eighth grade English teacher.

I've learned Sunday school can be really weird. Age 14.

I've learned balance in your life is important. Age 16.

I've learned Charlie actually knows a lot. Age 18.

I've learned Charlie is not as dumb as he looks. Age 16.

I've learned not to get kicked out of Sunday school, I might become a murderer. Age 15. My cautionary tale of Janos hits home.

I've learned nothing is funnier to boys than blowing milk out their nose. Age 14.

I've learned never to hold a cat and turn on the vacuum cleaner at the same time. Age 16. Now, there is wisdom for the ages.

I've learned you cannot hide spinach in milk. Mom always sees it. Age 15.

So goes the wisdom of teenagers. By the end of these sessions, we gained some knowledge, a few laughs, and I hope, a deeper appreciation of King Solomon's maxims.

Reflecting on Genesis and the rest of the Old Testament, I told them the books reflected a vengeful and jealous God and the history of the Jewish people, but the New Testament is much different. I urged them to read more of the Old Testament to get a feel for the Jewish history and traditions, but we would move to the New Testament for the remainder of our Bible studies.

Author as Sonny Bono during skit at Hope UMC

The wise fellow who coined the "Whoa! Man!" phrase for Adam waking to find Eve? Bryce became a senior team manager of a national financial services company. Definitely on the accomplished list.

CHAPTER NINE

Start with the Source

I wanted to make a point to the class of the complex history of the Bible we read today. There is no original bible in an obscure or well-known museum somewhere in the world, so I let my history degree lead me in relating this fact.

Making comparisons, I asked the class where one could find the Code of Hammurabi, one of the first listings of laws for a society in the history of the world, dating back 3,795 years. No one knew. I told the class they can see the Code in the Louvre Museum in Paris and remarked how one can go and read it today.

Next, I asked how many knew of the Magna Carta, the first document limiting the powers of the King of England back in 1215. One obviously well-read teen raised a hand. When I asked where one could go and read it, again, no one knew, so I asked if any traveled to London. A few hands went up.

"Did you go to the British Museum, the British Library? I believe you can find it there." I tried to make all this sound interesting while developing my thought.

I then asked where one could find the founding documents of the United States of America. More blank looks, but a few glimmers of hope in the eyes of some. "Uh, Washington, D. C.?" One intrepid soul spoke up.

We talked about the Archives of the United States of America on the mall between the Capitol building and the Lincoln Memorial housing the Declaration of Independence and the Constitution. I told them any of us can go and read those original documents.

I told the class we would spend the year studying the Bible, also known as scripture, one of the four pillars of the Methodist Quadrilateral. Then I asked if anyone knew where we could find the original Bible.

"Jerusalem?" One timid and not so confident, response.

"No, but that is a good guess," I acknowledged.

I went on to tell the class I used a trick question. We cannot produce the original documents for either the Old or New Testaments. There is no place to go and read the original documents of our faith, but the power of the stories and witnesses keep the message alive for us. We can see originals of other documents influencing our culture, society, and way of life, but not the Bible.

We moved on to discuss the fact the Bible, despite being a perennial best seller, for many, remains a book unread. It sits on a shelf or even in a prominent place in their homes, but few read it regularly. I am no Biblical scholar, but I read most of it and completed several college level courses on various biblical topics.

Since the Bible holds an almost mythical position in world literature, as an "all-knowing-word-of-God-ultimate-truths," kind of book, how does one approach teens about this magnificent work? I thought my undergraduate degree in history might help. I planned to give the class some background and historical information, and then move into a deeper study of its contents.

I finally made the point and hoped to set up the next several sessions. Knowing we do not have the original documents raises the natural question. What do we have? Copies, hand-copied documents we call manuscripts exist, but these raise questions about mistakes, errors, and corrections, especially if it involved an untrained or unsophisticated copyist.

We know of over 5,000 Greek manuscripts for the New Testament. Some are fragments of papyrus from Egypt. Others were written in Armenian, Coptic, and Syriac languages. One of the earliest documents contains lines from John 18 and dates from the second century CE, circa 125 CE, within thirty or forty years of John's gospel. Scholars also identified vellum, or animal skin, copies from the fourth century CE, but most documents date to the Middle Ages—the seventh century CE.

All the copies have mistakes because only a few contain the exact same wording. This fact led to a methodology called Textual Criticism, a process to determine the original text by comparing all the variants and choosing the one closest to the original. This surprised most teens in our class and reinforced my goal of getting each person to think for themselves about their faith.

Next, I asked the class how they thought people wrote the Bible in the first place. Answers varied:

"God told someone to write it down."

"Some inspired person wrote down the stories."

"The authors knew God and wanted to write down what they knew."

"You are all correct, to a point," I then moved into different theories of Biblical authorship and told the class each theory has followers and some who follow a combination of the theories.

The Verbal Inspiration theory identifies a process whereby the authors took mechanical dictation from God and humankind took it down exactly as God laid it out. This one sounds a lot like your comment "God told them to write it down."

The Natural Inspiration theory tells us humans achieved inspiration on their own from God's presence or events and wrote down the ideas and stories as best they could, using their own talents and intellect.

The Combination-Verbal theory indicates the personalities of God and man intertwine, but God dictates the story. Even though a man chooses the words and structure, they reflect the thoughts and words of God.

The Dynamic theory states God revealed herself and her truth to humankind, then humankind, considering its own experience and vocabulary, accurately recorded the revelation.

We closed the discussion of these theories with the Mythic theory. This theory states the Bible comes from humans, perhaps inspired to illustrate a universal truth, such as love. In this theory, humankind made up the stories. Other than perhaps providing the inspiration, God stays out of the process.

The varied theories and ideas surprised some teens. Some admitted to not thinking about it but expressed respect for the different ways scholars went about the puzzle.

Soon we touched on the nomenclature of the Bible. First, the word bible means "books" and the word itself, provided clues into its contents. We reviewed the types of books found in the Bible: History, Story, Proverbial, Devotion, Psalms, Poetry, Prophecy, Novels, and Narrative accounts. These theories of how we got the Bible and the breadth of the different books included also surprised most teenagers.

The class discussed how many Bible stories appear miraculous and frankly, hard to accept at face value. This set up a session on how to approach reading and study of the Bible. In a similar way to several theories about how the Bible came to be written, we can use different ways to look at its writings.

I gave the class this account of a young boy in Sunday school hearing the story of Moses parting the Red Sea for the children of Israel to escape Egypt. When the young boy got home, his Father asked him what he learned in Sunday school. The boy replied they learned about Moses leading the Israelites across the Red Sea.

"Tell me how the story went," the father directed.

"Well, Moses got on the walkie-talkie and called in the Israeli army engineers. They built these portable dams across the sea and then pumped all the water over to the other side of the dams. Then he called in the helicopters to come fly over the area until they dried the land. The people all got across when Pharaoh's army came after them. Moses waited until the army got in the middle of the dry land and then called the air force to come bomb the dams so the water would rush back in and drown the army. And that is how Moses led them across the Red Sea."

"Hmmm," the Father replied. "I don't believe that is what they told you in Sunday school."

"Well, you're right, but if I told you what they told us, you wouldn't believe that story either!"

The class laughed, but also saw the truth in the little boy's thought process.

We reviewed different ways to study the Bible. First, we covered the idea one can read the stories as allegory or parable. Essentially, the persons, objects, and/or animals in the stories each represent a moral or religious principle or standard and we can all learn from these.

Then we talked about the literal reading of the Bible. Here everything is literal. It means exactly what it says, regardless of improbability. While simple and straightforward, in my view a literal read is difficult for many parts of the Bible.

I told the class they could study the text as legend. These stories came down from the past, may have an element of truth to them, and many people believe them, but no one can verify or authenticate them.

Reading the Bible as myth is another way to approach the text. One can treat it as a real or fictional story appealing to the consciousness of a people by embodying its cultural ideals and/or ethos. One cannot prove the elements of the stories.

We covered a dogmatic approach. This allows the reader to use the text to prove his or her beliefs. Here one makes up his or her mind and uses the text to justify what is already believed.

An historical approach allows the reader to look at the date written, to whom written, and its purpose. In addition, one looks to the environmental, governmental, and societal situations present when written. The text can indicate what God said or how God reacted at different times and situations and use them for our learning today.

To wrap these into a bundle, we talked about a flexible approach to the study of the Bible. This allows us to use various methods during the study: literal or contextual, legend or history, and man's interpretation of what happened versus God's revelation.

I candidly told the class I relied on the historical and flexible approaches. They work for my mindset and logic, but they may not work for everyone.

Bringing this introduction of our Bible into practical terms for teenagers, I gave the class some ideas to keep in mind while reading the text. I urged them to read the Bible seriously and seek to learn something applicable to their life or situation.

Below are some of the ideas I listed.

The Bible text is in lay terms, not scientific or technical wording. It uses the language of common people over the centuries. We can look for the principle involved in the situations covered in the stories. We can look for the immediate and the higher connection. What does it mean to you? What do you think the author is telling us?

Ask yourself if the stories are meant literally or symbolically. Is the principle or truth presented hyperbolically or literally?

I also urged the class to think of the Bible as a guide for us today. In the spiritual sense, the Bible can provide a way for us to become closer to God, to learn God's will for us. It can bring us closer to our sense of God.

When I mentioned the Bible could be a source of liberation, some questioned this because they did not perceive anything holding them. This allowed us to discuss how all people can feel fear, loneliness, and separation from God. This got us into talking about freedom from sin and death—heavy topics for any of us, especially young folks.

Finally, I urged the class to use the Bible as a resource to learn about God's people and the stories of God's interaction with humans. More importantly, I asked them to examine what these stories could mean to them personally. I told them these approaches, methods, and concepts could serve them in their studies now and throughout their lives. This became my fervent prayer.

CHAPTER TEN

Who Am I?

I wanted the class members to read the Bible and relate its stories to their lives. Maybe it could help them with those big questions: Who am I? What is my purpose? What should I do with my life?

Going into my seventh decade on this good earth gave me a realization of the human lifespan a fourteen-year-old lacks. In the last decade of teaching, I accumulated more years teaching the class than the students' ages. The thought shook me when I asked the year of their birth and the replies came back 2001, 2003 and so forth.

In other ways, associating with teens each Sunday kept me young and learning about the latest technology or Internet sensation. I thought Facebook a waste of time until the class urged me to use it to communicate with them. They taught me about social media and helped me through the operational concepts and techniques for a smart phone.

They also showed me how to keep digital files for photographs. Since I served as Historian for the church, this helped tremendously, even though I felt they dragged me kicking and screaming into the twenty-first century.

In the early years, questions in class without ready answers waited until the next week to allow research for the answers. Toward the end of my teaching gig, those questions prompted some to pull out smart phones, repeat the question to the phone, and then let the class hear the answer. Amazing technology for a person who turned six-years-old before his family owned a television.

My recognition of time and everyone's search for answers gave me an idea. As mentioned earlier, this turned into a year-long study called: Who Am I? Where Am I Going? What Tools Will I Take With Me? And What Will I Do When Something Goes Wrong? We started with some simple questions.

I addressed the class and asked their age. We went around the room and everyone stated their age. Then, I asked them to think back ten years. How old were you then? Ages 4, 5, 6, 7, or 8 represented a time warp from their current ages. I next asked who made decisions for them at that age. They all admitted none made their own decisions at those ages. Their parents made most decisions for them, and rightfully so.

To acknowledge them and encourage them, I noted how far they advanced in the past ten years. I followed up to ask who made such decisions today. This produced a mixed bag of answers.

The seventeen- and eighteen-year-olds said they made most of the decisions on a day-to-day basis. They had independence on what to wear, what to eat, when to study, choosing friends, and so on. The fourteen- and fifteen-year-olds were getting there but lacked the same degree of independence as the older teens. Parents still made a large percentage of the decisions for these teens, but they gained more independence each month. The sixteen-year-olds got special recognition since this age allowed them to get learner's permits followed by a real driver's license.

To push the illustration further, I asked them to think about who will make decisions for them ten years from today. You would have thought I threw down a gantlet. The thought of the coming self-determination usually brought smiles to their faces and a little swagger to their step. In ten short years, they must make nearly all decisions for themselves. Within ten years, no one admitted expecting parents to make their decisions. I told them they would be shocked at how quickly the ten years would pass.

I drove the idea home by telling them in ten years most of them will be out of college, perhaps married, maybe parents themselves, and we all hoped, gainfully employed. By then, they should know who they are, where they are going, what tools they have with them, and what they plan to do when something goes wrong.

This set up our next discussion. I asked the class to use me for the first example. Who is Charlie?

Some of the answers put forward included: lawyer, father, photographer, teacher, American, Christian, male, good guy, Marine.

"Excellent, all those descriptions tell us something about me, but let's dig a little deeper." I continued the line of questions. "Who knows where the Ledbetter family originated?"

"Texas," came an early reply. Turning from the board toward the class, I said, "I came from there, but what about my ancestors? Where did they come from?"

"England, Germany, somewhere in Europe." More quick replies.

"Getting closer. The story I heard indicated the original Ledbetters came from the borderlands between England and Scotland, and then moved to Ireland before coming to America. This makes me of Scots-Irish descent. On my mother's side, Gowdys and Harpers, both Irish."

We talked about how everyone's family includes ancestors and their history becomes part of our history. We went around the room asking about the national origin of their families. The answers covered the globe. We named England, Germany, France, Ireland, Denmark, Holland, Spain, Italy, Hungary, Greece, most of the European countries. In addition, we named Mexico, Guatemala, Brazil, Australia, Japan, the Philippines, Vietnam, and Korea.

The far-flung origins of our ancestors surprised us and allowed each person a moment of attention to talk about their family. Many knew of family stories of hardship and sacrifice others endured so we could enjoy the advantages of today. All of us recognized the blessing of living in the modern United States of America.

Next, I asked what else identified me and reminded them someone called me a Christian. Most of us identified as Christian. This brought on a deeper discussion about Christians in general. I asked if they considered Catholics, Presbyterians, Mormons, Greek Orthodox, and Episcopal/Anglicans as Christians. We got some puzzled looks, but most agreed these were also Christians, like the Methodists. I talked about the early church as related in Acts of the Apostles, the Roman sanctioning of the church during the later empire years, and how the Reformation led to many of the variations we see today.

I stressed recognition of Jesus as the Christ or Son of God as the main tie for these different communities of faith. We may have different worship styles, rituals, and sacraments, but the underlying theme remains, Christ centers our faith.

One student asked which factor is most important to who we are, our heritage and family history, or our faith? Some argued both are equally important. Others insisted our faith, our identity as a Christian constituted the most important thing. For once, I did not lead the discussion, but let it play out. A fun lesson for us all.

Being one to seek consensus and avoid confrontation, I spoke up for both factors, but I leaned toward our faith edging out our heritage as a primary identifier. I told the class how they acted on their faith would determine more about who they become than their family history.

The question of who am I produced a month's worth of discussion and set us up for the next question: Where am I going? I returned to myself as an example. "Did I have a direction to my life at your age?"

It took some encouraging, but the class delivered. "You went to college. You got a law degree. You planned a career." They knew these achievements said something about me.

"At your age, I wanted to be a professional basketball player. It became my main goal for a while, but after playing in college, I realized I lacked enough talent. This led me to finishing college and planning for law school. My father's example as a lawyer and judge led me to those plans. But, sometimes, you need to readjust your goals."

They also remembered I needed to adjust my life to keep some balance. I felt proud they remembered we need to work on our intellectual, physical, and spiritual sides. We discussed setting goals, having ambitions and aspirations. Most of the class members wanted to attend college, a few held clear ideas about a profession, but some kept their options open.

We talked about the seriousness of choosing a mate and deciding to have a family. Following a societal trend of the past twenty years, I told the class I supported the idea of marriage later than earlier generations. I told them I married a couple of weeks before my twenty-second birthday, and in retrospect, more maturity would have served me better.

I also asked about a different dimension to the question. Where am I going, in a broader sense, can mean what kind of person I wish to be. Goals and ambitions are great and serve us well, but on a deeper level, we get to decide what kind of person we become. I believe in the concept of free will for individuals. We can choose our ethics, morals, ideas of justice, and personal standards. We must make decisions on how we live, act or react to issues. I tried to impress upon the class how the next ten years will produce many events and decisions that shape who they become.

I used the familiar story of the fellow who walks down the road and falls into a hole. The next day, the fellow is more careful, but walks down the same road and falls into the same hole. The next day, same result. On the fourth day, the fellow decides to walk down a different road.

I urged the class to consider their free will carefully when it comes to their Christian faith. I believe we choose to follow Christ and being sincere in the decision requires us to try each day to live a Christ-centered life. By doing this, our faith sustains us and guides us for the rest of our lives.

Urging the class to understand decisions they make now affect their attitudes later, I told them now is the best time to involve their faith in all decisions. I revisited my experience with Janos and the incidents in his life. In my view, most of his troubles came from personal decisions he made as a teenager.

To point out the difficulty we all face in making good, Christ-like decisions, I used an exercise to put tough decisions before the class. Before we jumped into the exercise, we read aloud *James 1:2–8 "Consider it pure joy, my brothers, whenever you face trials of many kinds, because you know that the testing of your faith develops perseverance. Perseverance must finish its work so that you may be mature and complete, not lacking anything. If any of you lacks wisdom, let him ask God . . . and it will be given him."*

And, *James 4:13–17 "Now listen, you who say, 'Today or tomorrow we will go into this or that city, and spend a year there, carry on business and make money.' Why, you do not even know what will happen tomorrow. What is your life? You are a mist that appears for a little while and then vanishes. Instead, you ought to say, 'If it is the Lord's will, we will live and we shall do this or that.' As it is, you boast and brag. All such boasting is evil. Anyone then, who knows the good he ought to do and doesn't do it, sins."*

We then continued with the exercise, which I called: Decisions, Decisions.

You are the member of the Board of Directors of a large corporation. It has a factory in the small country of Ledsland. The factory employs 400 workers who are so poor they barely survive with the money your company pays them. The factory produces pajamas for small children and is wildly successful.

One of the reasons the factory is profitable for your company is the pajamas lack flame retardant treatment. To provide this treatment would eliminate the cost advantages your company enjoys in the market. You recently learned worldwide, 1 in 10,000 children using your company's pajamas receive severe burns each year. These burns could be avoided if your company applied the flame-retardant treatment.

Charlie Gotbucks, the president, strongly opposes anything that adds to the cost of your products. He points out the added costs could cause the factory to close and the 400 employees and their families would return to subsistence living. Besides, the burns only occurred for 1 in 10,000.

You want the Board of Directors to discuss this and a vote to go on record about how they feel the company should proceed. What are your thoughts, how would you vote, and what beliefs or principles support your position?

The class jumped into a wide-ranging discussion. Some participated in debate at school and used those skills to push one side or the other. Everyone agreed the factory made a positive impact for employees, but regretted the burns to any child, regardless of the statistics.

The exercise set up a conundrum, one not easily resolved, but it got the class into the issues. One of the most interesting ideas proposed: cut Charlie Gotbucks' pay in an amount equal to the cost of the flame-retardant treatments. We learned our decisions matter. Goal accomplished.

Next, we moved into: What tools we will take with us on life's journey? Since we talked about free will and our faith, I stressed faith as the first tool in one's toolbox.

I echoed James' words regarding anyone who lacks wisdom "let him ask God … and it will be given him." I stressed a community of faith usually comes with one's faith. This can be an extension of the faith tool. Sometimes within the community, we support others and sometimes we receive the support. For most of us, the community of faith consists of our family, our parents, and our friends. In addition to the community of faith as a tool, we discussed our friends as another tool that, even though included in our community of faith, could be considered a separate and distinct tool to take with us.

The class provided good ideas on what makes a good friend. Some of the things mentioned included: they can keep a secret, they love you, they don't judge you, they support you, they can criticize you without being mean about it, and they help you make decisions. Some took the Boy Scouts' approach: a friend is trustworthy, loyal, helpful, friendly, courteous, and so forth.

We discussed friends as mentioned in *John 15:12–14 "My command is this: Love each other as I have loved you. Greater love has no one than this that one lay down his life for his friends."*

Since most of us do not lay down our lives for others, we can also look at this as a call for service. I asked how we might dedicate our lives for others. The class quickly pointed out physicians, nurses, emergency medical personnel, teachers, ministers, and members of our military.

Next, we talked about another tool for use the rest of their lives: prayer. This topic also covered several sessions and allowed us to dig deeper in the concept and practice of prayer. I suggested prayer is a natural thing and hoped it came easily. At its base level, prayer provides communication with our best friend—God. It rewards us by allowing us into God's presence, allowing us to experience God's power, and letting us experience God's guidance. What a powerful concept.

In addition, prayer allows us to build our community of faith through corporate or group prayer. It brings us together with others who love God and reminds us we are not alone. As *Matthew 18: 20* reminds us *"for where two or three come together, there am I with them."* It also reminds us of the power of prayer in our lives, again, *Matthew 7:7 "Ask and it will be given to you; seek and you will find; knock and the door will be opened to you."*

I also stressed prayer is a privilege, not a duty. A disciplined approach to prayer delivers great results by helping us with difficult times or during moments of indecision. We talked about the concept of prayer, one based on the idea God is good, cares for us, and wants to communicate with us. I wanted the class to know the power of this tool.

Winding up our discussion on tools, we revisited the Bible, one of the four pillars of the quadrilateral. We covered how regular Bible reading and study paid dividends and tied us to our community of faith. I told the class how I read and then re-read parts of the Bible over several years, and often I discerned something different each time, hoping to impress on them how Bible reading touches us repeatedly.

To conclude our yearlong study, I asked the class to conceive a large circular track. We humans are moving around the track. Regardless of where we are on the track, others are ahead or behind us. We can go to those folks for guidance when something goes wrong. Most likely, their experience could help us. This tied into another question. What are you going to do when something goes wrong?

I reminded them my life story included a loss of a loved one, anger at God, emphasis on one thing instead of keeping a balance in my life, and unhappiness. In addition to revisiting the story, I told the class of the deaths of three of my sisters and my parents. These painful experiences come with human existence. The crucial thing in this process is what you do when they occur.

Author, second from left with class 2004

When things go wrong, what do you do? Death, loss, troubles, and illness in our lives present a time to return to the idea of who you are. What are your ethics, morals, beliefs? Where are you going? Are you pursuing a Christ-like life, living out your faith? Remember the tools along with you: your faith, your community of faith, your friends, prayer, and the Bible. Use them to the fullest extent possible. I believe these points allow us to endure the troubles we face and urged the class to remember and use them.

Oh, the fellow who asked about the most important characteristic of who am I—family history or faith? This young man became an Army officer responsible for the well-being of over 300 servicemen and women. Another for the A list.

CHAPTER ELEVEN

Am I the Anti-Christ?

We next focused on the New Testament. It, in my opinion, is a revered and fascinating document. I learned to regard it as the most significant book in the history of western civilization.

Understanding the American culture requires knowing something about the New Testament. Our political scene includes many references to its influence, and some would say direction, about many social issues: slavery, women, homosexuals, same sex marriage and so on. All touch on fertile grounds for young minds.

Of course, the lawyer and history major in me dictated some preliminary groundwork for approaching a study of the New Testament. I believe it to be a source of inspiration for the faithful, but at the same time a source for studying its cultural impact in western civilization. One must acknowledge the Christian church in the development of western civilization. Avoiding its influence on art and literature is impossible.

I also told the class we can look at the New Testament from a historical perspective. This approach allows a view of a secular scholar—a historian—not of a believer, for the writings of the early Christian era.

Because the topic, a survey of the New Testament, encompassed so much material, I planned lessons to cover a class year, roughly coinciding with the school year.

I figured a pop quiz would give me a baseline for the class's knowledge of the New Testament and used it the first week of class. Here is the quiz we used: *

Within 100 years, the date of writing the New Testament?

The language used in the original New Testament?

Whose life dominates the subject matter of the first four books in the New Testament?

What are the first four books in the New Testament commonly called?

Many books in the New Testament are letters to individuals or churches. Another word for letter is?

Who wrote the New Testament called the Letter of James?

Who wrote 2nd Corinthians?

What book contains a history of the Apostles and early church?

Which book contains dreams, visions, monsters, and secret codes?

Who gets credit for writing the most books in the New Testament?

How many books in the New Testament?

Who wrote the book of First Charles?

Two authors who wrote one of the gospels also wrote other books in the New Testament. Can you name one? Two?

Which books of the New Testament did Jesus write?

Name the books known as the Synoptic Gospels?

What are the Gnostic gospels?

Why does the Bible exclude the Gnostic gospels?

As anticipated, the answers were all over the place, the most common: "I don't know." Many knew the first four books as the Gospels, some knew James wrote the Letter of James, or at least, sensed he wrote it. Many also knew First Charles does not appear in the New Testament, but the rest of the quiz drew blanks. This did not surprise me. God forbid I needed to pass this test at seventeen.

We started by talking about the approved or canonical books in the New Testament. Learning the listing of twenty-seven books remained unsettled until the fourth century surprised most class members. Then church leaders confirmed the list of books to include the canonical gospels, Acts of the Apostles, letters from early Christians, and Revelation.

The gospels supplied a natural start. The class knew the gospels describe the life, teachings, and death and resurrection of Jesus. Most knew the familiar stories of Jesus' life and many of the parables, but not much else. The common answer to the first gospel written? Matthew, of course. Wrong!

Mark, the first gospel written, allowed us to touch on journalistic practices. The class knew about the standard format for newspaper or magazine articles providing the Who, What, When, Where, and How of the story. We talked about how Mark followed those guidelines. His is the shortest, contains nothing about Jesus' birth, and focuses on the last four years of Jesus' life.

Mark wrote to identify Jesus' role and showed him as a miracle man, the Messiah/Christ. It also surprised the class to learn our earliest extant copy of Mark ends at Chapter16: Verse 8. Verses 9 through 20 came into the text later and are currently included as accepted text.

Mark provides a rich account of Jesus' life and death and molded early beliefs of Jesus as an unexpected Messiah. Mark writes Jesus' suffering and death as neither accidental nor incidental to his role as Messiah. Mark's readers, as disciples of Jesus, must take up the cross and follow. It gave us the challenge of what our faith really means to us and what responsibilities come with it.

Matthew provided a view of Jesus as the Jewish Messiah, but probably not the view of an eyewitness. Mathew saw the Gospel of Mark for reference and probably another source referred to as "Q." from the German word for source—Quelle. He retells some of the stories of Mark but adds new ones. Matthew, traditionally known as a Jewish tax collector, writes from a Jewish perspective. He posits Jesus is the Messiah, the son of God, who condemned the way the Jews practiced their religion during Jesus' time. He adds emphasis of Jesus as a Jew: the genealogy of Jesus back through David to Abraham and presents Jesus as the Jewish Messiah.

Matthew is rich with Jesus' teachings. The stories show Jesus interpreting the Law of Moses and urging his followers to follow the letter of the law, but also the spirit of the law. He outlines Jesus' opposition to Jewish leaders as hypocrites who know the right things to do, but who failed to do them. We returned to Matthew later for more study of the Lord's Prayer and the Beatitudes.

Most sources claim Matthew and Luke date from between 80 and 85 CE and the authors probably saw Mark's gospel and the Q document. However, Luke presents the gospel stories from yet another perspective. Luke is unknown to history other than as a travel companion of Paul and as the author of Acts of the Apostles. He stresses Jesus as the savior of the world who came for all men, not only for the Jews.

Luke begins his gospel differently from Mark and Matthew in that he uses a "preface" style similar to other ancient documents. Because Luke's phrasing contains "wanting a true account," one can infer he wants to set the story straight. He most likely felt the earlier gospels lacked some details or emphases. Instead of the Jewish genealogy of Jesus as found in Matthew, Luke traces Jesus back to Adam. This reinforces the idea Jesus came for all humankind.

Luke takes pains to stress everything in Jesus' life goes according to God's plan. He avoids the apocalyptic notion the end of the world is near and goes on to lay out the idea of the Kingdom of God is for everyone, but it did not happen right away. He also stresses God wanted the message to go to the gentiles (all men). This theme continues in Acts of the Apostles.

Many in the class identified with the strong social agenda in Luke. His emphasis on the concerns of the poor and needy resonated with many of the teens. The women also liked the passages supporting the rights of women.

The class took interest in the variety and richness of the book. They paid more attention than I feared they might as we covered the material. Only a few of the class members knew about the similarities and differences in the Gospels. They attended private schools, Catholic, and Dutch Reformed Church. When such members were in our classes, we took advantage of their schooling and gave those students the opportunity to help with the lessons. They often added to the discussions and lent depth or nuance to things I prepared. Having them in class gave me blessings.

The Synoptic Gospels took a couple of sessions. With this unfamiliar term, I attempted some humor by introducing the term as the One-eyed Gospels. Furrowed brows and surprise followed my announcement we wanted to talk about the One-eyed Gospels.

Synoptic literally means "seen together" or "taking a common view." I took some license to call it "seen with one eye" or the One-eyed Gospels. Talking through the word and my take on it, allowed the class to see how the concept applied to the first three Gospels—Matthew, Mark, and Luke. These Gospels tell many of the same stories in Jesus' life.

Many readers over the ages recognized this and scholars created a classic reference called Gospel Parallels. This book allows its readers to view corresponding passages in parallel columns on the page. Many benefited from this tool as a revealing way to compare and contrast the gospel texts. My edition, copyrighted in 1979, also includes full non-canonical parallels, such as those found in Gospel of the Ebionites, Gospel of the

Hebrews, Gospel of the Nazaraeans, Gospel of Peter, and the Gospel of Thomas.

We spent some time reviewing the book, *Gospel Parallels, A Synopsis of the First Three Gospels,* edited by Burton H. Throckmorton, Jr., Thomas Nelson Publishers, reading how a familiar story from the New Testament reads differently depending on which book you review. In a way, this helped the class see the depth and nuance to the stories. It also helped open eyes to the topic.

The fourth gospel, John, took us in another direction. We started with John's opening words, *"In the beginning, there was the Word, and the Word was with God." John 1:1.* This prologue or opening hymn presents a different look compared to the other three gospels. The style is more meditative or reflective, unlike the others.

Written last, it takes a different emphasis and tone throughout. John is similar to the other gospels because it contains many familiar stories, but differs by leaving out Jesus' birth, baptism, temptation, parables, the last supper, and trial by Jewish authorities.

On the other hand, it presents Jesus' startling deeds—turning water into wine, raising Lazarus from the dead, and so forth. Being the last one written, perhaps it means to clarify the reason for Jesus' life. In the synoptic gospels Jesus does not prove his identity, in fact refuses to do acts to prove who he is. In John's account, Jesus does this by using the miracles or signs to prove his identity.

John eschews the parables, but talks of who Jesus is, whence he came, how he relates to God and how he is the one sent by God to bring salvation. John suggests eternal life exists already, not something in the future, and Jesus existed from the beginning with God.

John goes to great lengths to lay out Jesus' sayings. We sometimes call these the I am listings. "I am—Messiah, Bread of Life, Not of this World, Before Abraham, Light of the World, God's Son, Resurrection and the Life, The Way-Truth-Life, and the True Vine." Most heard these before but never stopped to think they came from one gospel and not all.

We completed our study of John and then circled back to Matthew, the Sermon on the Mount, and the Beatitudes, often called the "blessed" or "happy" statements in Matthew, Chapter 5. A beatitude reflects a state of happiness or utmost bliss, sometimes referred to as complete happiness promised because of some virtue. Matthew lays out eight qualities of Christian perfection along with a promise of future blessings instead of current rewards.

Matthew 5:3 "Blessed are the poor in spirit; for theirs is the Kingdom of heaven." The poor in this quote represent the destitute, those barely surviving, who know their spiritual poverty and stand humbly before God. They rely on God. Their reward comes as the Kingdom of God, not with a worldly, nationalistic kingdom. The Kingdom of God can become a present possession, here and now.

Matthew 5:4 "Blessed are those who mourn, for they will be comforted." The Greek words indicate mourning as though for the dead, the bitterest sorrow of life. Matthew's words may mean those desperately sorry for the sadness and suffering of the world will find the joy of God.

Matthew 5:5 "Blessed are the meek, for they will inherit the earth." Humble ones, not those lacking courage, know their own weakness and need. Those humble before God will inherit not only the blessedness of heaven but will share in the kingdom of God upon the earth.

Matthew 5:6 "Blessed are those who hunger and thirst for righteousness, for they will be filled." Those who seek what is moral, what is right, look for righteousness. The text refers to those who go hungry and thirsty, as a standard to ask how much do you want what is moral? The Christian experiences a God-given hunger and thirst for righteousness that only God can fill.

Matthew 5:7 "Blessed are the merciful, for they will be shown mercy." This elegant saying clearly shows one must forgive, to gain forgiveness. One must get into another's skin, see through his eyes, not just show sympathy from outside. The Christian shows mercy not to receive mercy, but because God gives us mercy.

Matthew 5:8 "Blessed are the pure in heart, for they will see God." The Greek words connote a clean, unmixed, unadulterated heart and require self-examination. A Christian must possess pure motives for actions, and if so, they will see God.

Matthew 5:9 "Blessed are the peacemakers for they will be called the sons of God." The Greek and Hebrew terms refer to peace as more than the absence of trouble/war, but as a state capable of enjoying all good things. They receive blessings because they do God-like work with all humankind.

Matthew 5:10–12 "Blessed are those who are persecuted because of righteousness, for theirs is the kingdom of heaven. Blessed are you when people insult you, persecute you and falsely say all kinds of evil against you because of me. Rejoice and be glad for great is your reward in heaven, for in the same way they persecuted the prophets who were before you." Matthew makes it clear Jesus knows his followers will come into conflict with the world in which they live.

The class enjoyed the Beatitudes. Reading and discussing these blessings gave all of us a deeper appreciation for the early Christians and whetted our appetites to find out more about the New Testament.

After our review of the gospels, we moved onto Acts of the Apostles. I told the class we would touch on it, but a full study came with our study of Paul's life. We reviewed Pentecost and the development of the early community of believers before moving onto Romans. I told the class most of Paul's letters went to specific church communities and dealt with local issues. With Romans, he takes a different approach and lays out his understanding of the Christian gospel. He focuses on salvation by faith, a theme we explore further during our study of Paul's life, and salvation comes to all—Jews and gentiles alike—and is apart from doing the works of the law.

Paul uses two models to structure his thinking, a legal or judicial model and a participation model. To keep the class' eyes from glazing over, I tried to keep Paul's models short and lively, but still cover the ideas. The judicial model relates sin as an act of disobedience (not following the law) and the penalty, death. However, Christ paid the penalty for all and therefore, faith and trusting acceptance of this fact, provides salvation to us. The participation model implies sin is equal to an evil cosmic power that enslaves humans. Again, the penalty is death, but Christ died for all of us to negate the penalty.

To Paul this meant Christ broke the power of death and we participate in the salvation by baptism. We talked about the implications of this for Judaism. It implied the secondary nature of the law. This went against centuries of Jewish teaching and probably produced Jesus' issues with the Jewish authorities.

We mentioned the Pauline epistles briefly. I told the class to expect a deeper reading of them when we went into Paul's life for a full year's study. The class soaked up the gospels and enjoyed Romans but showed some fatigue or lack of focus with Hebrews. Turned out, they wanted to get to the most enigmatic of all mystery books—The Revelation of John. To keep things moving and to end the year on a bang, we hustled through Hebrews.

I told the class the early church thought Paul wrote Hebrews, later scholars not so much. The book dealt with Christianity's relationship with Judaism. The essence boiled down to Christ as superior to everything in Judaism, the prophets, Moses, and the law. Hebrews also indicated Jesus fulfilled the scriptures and made Judaism obsolete. The writer tells us by sending Jesus to live among us, God made a new covenant with the people. This new covenant made the laws laid out in the Old Testament no longer valid.

To end the year at a peak, we dove into Revelation, sometimes called the Apocalypse of John. John names himself as the author, but maybe not the apostle John because he relates seeing the Twelve Apostles in a vision but does not say he saw himself. Whoever wrote the book got his money's worth over the centuries because many used Revelation to predict the future. The first and second centuries saw the Apocalypse as a popular topic among Christians and Jews.

Some latch onto one or more bizarre visions told in Revelation and use them to predict all kinds of things. The class wanted to jump on this bandwagon and talk about one or another image.

I urged them to look at the book in its entirety, review the genre itself, and try to understand some of the symbols. This got us away from some of the specious claims and allowed a deeper look at the text.

One of the best discussions came with Chapter 13 where we read of a beast with ten horns and seven heads and the designation of the number of the beast as 6, 6, 6. The class told of zombie movies and supernatural thrillers that all referred to these 666 signs of the devil, evil, anti-Christ, whatever. We talked about gematria, the ancient practice of coding alphanumeric characters to reveal disparate items somehow related to each other. Using this for Revelation allowed a human name with eighteen letters (6+6+6) to represent something evil. Some interpretations used this to state 666 really meant the Roman Emperor Nero. John probably used a code to avoid further scrutiny from the Roman authorities.

To illustrate the slippery slope in this reasoning, I told the class this same process produced Hitler's given name or Ronald Wilson Reagan. A gasp suddenly broke my concentration. I looked in the direction of the voice and saw one of our members holding her hand over her mouth.

"What's the matter?" I asked.

"This could be me! I could be the anti-Christ." The young woman almost shouted, gaining everyone's attention.

"I always thought so." Her brother chimed in.

Now everyone paid attention. "What do you mean? I asked.

"Brooke Mariah Simson. That's my full name. 6, 6, 6 – I am in Revelation, and it's not good."

Everyone laughed and those sitting next to Brooke began moving away. Her younger brother laughed hardest and loudest. "I knew it, I knew it!" he added with a big smile.

"Brooke is one of the nicest people I know. I am sure she is not the anti-Christ, but you can see how people manipulate the text of Revelation." I tried to reassert some calm and control. Brooke's face still reflected puzzlement and concern.

I told the class I could not read Revelation as a prediction for twentieth or twenty-first century times. I saw the book in a first century context where Rome stood as the enemy of God and the early Christians. The anti-Christ could be the Emperor calling for persecution of Christians. I urged them to look at the book as a reassurance to the early Christians of the sovereignty of God and Christ. John's Revelation showed an end to their suffering.

Other classes came up with their own anti-Christs. It appears many kids have names with six letters for first, middle, and last names. I felt we gained a better view of the New Testament and a way to sleep at night after reading Revelation.

Yes, Brooke and her brother both belong on the accomplished list. Brooke attended the prestigious Colorado School of Mines and her brother went to the University of Colorado. In addition to being solid citizens and Christians, both received honors for their academic achievements.

*Answers to New Testament Quiz: 1) 80 – 120 CE, 2) Greek, 3) Jesus, 4) The Gospels, 5) Epistle, 6) James, the brother of Jesus, 7) Paul, 8) Acts of the Apostles, 9) The Revelation of John, 10) Paul, 11) 27, 12) No one, no such book, 13) Luke and John, 14) None, 15) Matthew, Mark & Luke, 16) Books contemporary with the Gospels, but not accepted into the official canon, 17) Church officials determined them lacking in tone, spirit, or contents when compared to Matthew, Mark, Luke and John.

CHAPTER TWELVE

Columbine Tragedy

On this particular Tuesday, I worked from home. Although I usually traveled out of town with my job, this week found me in Denver. The day started normally, but soon changed.

Most Coloradans, and many others who experienced it, Tuesday, April 20, 1999, carry deep emotional memories of an unbelievably horrific day. Even as I write this paragraph eighteen years later, the emotions of that day and the weeks following rise again in my consciousness.

My home office included a desk, phone with an 800-line, laptop computer, and a television. I used the morning to call business contacts. The television carried one of the stock market cable networks. I half-monitored it out of the corner of my eye while I worked the phone and computer.

Around noon, the phone rang with a call from one of my colleagues. "Is your family all right?"

"What?"

"Get on a news channel. A high school in Denver is under attack."

Columbine High School in suburban Denver came under attack by two students armed with bombs, shotguns, rifles, and an automatic machine gun. Within an hour after the attack began, thirteen people died and the two attackers took their own lives.

Confusion reigned during the first hours of the incident, no one seemed to know the number of shooters, the status of students and teachers, killed, wounded, missing, or what might happen next. Television coverage showed groups of police, sheriff's deputies, and emergency medical personnel surrounding the school, but little or no action.

The police followed a surround, observe, and contain strategy and this prevented them from entering the school to pursue the killers. Several hours passed. Long after the killers committed suicide, the extent of the carnage became clear. Parents, families, teachers, and the public found themselves in a suspended state awaiting news confirming something, anything, about their loved ones.

A personal interest linked my family, like so many others, to the event. Two nephews and a niece attended Columbine. My wife and I called family members trying to learn anything we could. We switched from channel to channel desperately looking for any tidbit of new developments.

Fortunately, two from our family left the campus for lunch and missed the danger. The grace of God spared the other nephew despite being in the immediate area of the main attacks. During the shooting and bomb throwing, teachers steered him and others away from the shooters down to an exit, and away from the building. When the other nephew and niece returned for afternoon classes, officials surrounded the school and prohibited access.

Those two joined the others anxiously trying to learn any news. Early suppositions about motives ranged from victims of bullying taking revenge, a pair of outcasts seeking publicity, two teens fascinated by violent video games, Goths or other cult-like devotees lashing out, and a nebulous group, called the Trench Coat Mafia, wreaking terror on the school. For most of us, nothing could explain how such a thing happened.

Months later, investigations and analyses attributed the senseless killing to one psychopath acting on a grandiose, inflated sense of superiority; an almost messianic complex. This person influenced another, who suffered from depression and low self-esteem, to join him in the attacks.

The shock and horror of the day reverberated through Denver, the nation, and around the world for months, even years to come. In the days after the attack, many churches held impromptu prayer vigils where thousands attended. I called our senior pastor to discuss how we might discuss the happenings of the week with our senior high class.

I began searching for ways to discuss this unimaginable event because I knew the teens would want and need, a way to process the events. Most of our teens attended the close by Cherry Creek High School, but the class included members from all over the metropolitan area. Most, through sports affiliations and family connections, knew kids who attended Columbine.

Luckily, the senior pastor agreed to join our class for the upcoming Sunday. I felt someone trained in grief counseling and familiar with how to talk with someone during an emotional and/or faith crisis could help the class deal with this terrible event.

He gave me some pointers over the phone as we discussed how to proceed. He mentioned how shock and disbelief became common for many and we needed to acknowledge it, not pretend it did not exist. For young people in particular, the acknowledgement usually validates their feelings and encourages them to talk about what bothers them.

I felt better because the conversation reminded me of my early instincts about teaching teenagers: acknowledge them, encourage them, and love them. He continued by saying situations like the Columbine killings often create fear and anxiety because people feel they lack control over their lives. He indicated our first job would be to support the class members by listening to them and giving them some pointers for dealing with their emotions.

We discussed how to conduct the class. He felt we should encourage everyone to seek out friends for talking through the grief. He also thought the class provided a good example of friends they could rely on for support. He agreed to take the lead and to encourage the class not to grieve alone, seek out others for help, and to take care of themselves by eating better, getting exercise, and pursuing creative activities.

We agreed on some of the talking points he mentioned and agreed to stress God's love for all while doing our best to allay fears for one's safety. Even with these tips and his experience, I worried about the challenges ahead.

On Sunday, I awoke with a pit in my stomach. Some of my own fears ran rampant and I wondered whether I could help others deal with their emotions. I attended the early service as usual but fretted through the worship. Thoughts of talking with the class right after the service occupied my mind.

Because of the week's events, our class doubled in size. Teens and parents looked to their faith for solace and comfort. Many families made a point of attending worship services and our class swelled accordingly. The classroom overflowed, about thirty of us bunched together in a room designed for twenty at the most. Several teens shared a chair or sat on top of each other as we filled the room. I skipped the usual practice of taking roll and seeking contributions, but deliberately and with some ceremony, lit the candle in the middle of the room. I wanted to remind the class of God's presence with us and paused for several seconds before speaking.

"Thank you for being here today." I cautiously began. "A community of faith like ours can help us in times like this. For obvious reasons, we will scrap our planned lesson and use this time to discuss what's on your mind. The pastor agreed to join and help us through the next hour."

The pastor spoke next. "For the most part, I want you to know God feels our pain and the pain of our community. I do not think this is God's will. God does not enjoy people suffering and our community is suffering. But, I am here to listen as much as anything."

Several seconds passed before a young lady spoke, "Why does God let something like this happen?"

The pastor and I exchanged looks before he spoke. "I believe God gives each of us free will. Free will allows people to make choices, do good things or do bad things. This week we saw two young men doing terrible things, by their choice. God doesn't control us like puppets, but God wants us to make decisions that reflect love, justice and understanding. We enjoy free will to do the right or wrong things." Right then, it thrilled me the pastor agreed to join us.

Someone asked about the Goths. Another said there were some at Creek and they were kooky.

I confessed a lack of knowledge about Goths but urged the class not to think poorly of people based on their looks. Looks can be deceptive. I stressed the error, for much of America's history, where we judged people by the color of their skin. I reminded them the situation remained murky about who played a role in the killings. Many times, teenagers searched for an identity. Maybe the killers here did.

One teen mentioned the Goths were looking for attention and were not typically violent; they simply wanted to be different and get people to notice them.

Someone asked about jocks and bullying. I mentioned my sports experience did not include bullying. If anything, we picked on each other more than we picked on non-jocks. I asked if they saw a different pattern today. Most did not and we agreed to wait until we knew more about what happened before we pursued this as a reason for the attacks.

The pastor told us he identified with the music/drama clique when he attended high school. He admitted dressing in tie-dye shirts and wearing long hair, mostly to look cool to colleagues. He recalled someone calling him a band geek, but never suffered any hazing or bullying.

Next, someone asked why the police did not storm the building with guns blazing to kill the bad guys before they killed more people. Both the pastor and I agreed we did not have a good explanation for the strategy, but in many situations like this, training kicks in and determines how officials react.

Someone mentioned this was real life, not a movie, and the police might hurt more people if they started shooting without knowing more. Someone joked and said this called for a Super Hero such as Superman or Batman, but those people only exist in fantasy. This broke the tension in the room, but only for a few seconds.

"I heard they asked one girl about being a Christian, and when she said 'yes,' they killed her.

All eyes turned to us for answers. The pastor replied some governments over the centuries, the Romans in particular, singled out early Christians for punishment because of their faith. He also said this rarely happens in the United States. He cautioned not to make too much of this story because the killers appeared to kill randomly, not looking only for Christians. He added the girl did an incredibly brave thing standing by her faith in the face of death and he hoped her family received comfort from their faith. He concluded by saying one's faith in eternal life, as he had, should provide comfort and peace in the face of death. He hoped the young girl killed at Columbine possessed this.

The group quietly pondered his words.

Several seconds later as the tension and anxiety hung in the room, one class member mentioned the killers murdered a black person, but she did not think the killers singled out black people.

I mentioned like the killing of a Christian, nothing indicated the killers singled out black people. The reports I saw and read indicated indiscriminate, not targeted killings. The class wondered if the killings contained some racial or religious element.

Another long pause ensued. We appeared lost in our thoughts. After several seconds, I broke the silence. "What can we say about our faith in the face of this terrible event?" I stood in the front and looked at the kids.

"Well, we believe God is love, isn't that what we believe?"

"But, how can we love the killers? Sure, we believe God is love and Jesus came to teach us how to love one another. But loving those two? I don't know how." Another jumped into the discussion.

The pastor stepped into the middle of the room. He paused a moment to make sure everyone paid attention. "Remember, our faith teaches us to love others as ourselves, even those who wrong us, turn the other cheek and all. It may not be popular to say this, but we need to pray for the families of the killers. They were someone's sons, grandsons—their families must be in shock, just as we are, and we need to keep them in our prayers.

We often do not know what to do, but at those times, we must reflect on our faith and fall back onto what it teaches us. Sometimes I must console a family whose infant child died. Nothing I can say will make things better, but I hope my presence and prayers for the family can lend some consolation, maybe not right then, but at some point. I think we must look at Columbine this way. Maybe someday we will understand why, but we can rely on our faith to help us get there."

"I feel sad and numb about the whole thing." A classmate added. Several nodded their heads in agreement but said nothing.

"What if something like this happened at our school?" A thought of many, but no one spoke of this fear until then. "Yeah, now I worry about it." Others joined.

I spoke about hearing a psychologist on television talking about this. He mentioned how with teens and an event like this, statistics about how unusual it is do not help. It is helpful though, to give direct suggestions about coping. One could talk with friends, family, or school officials about fears. He also encouraged everyone to speak up if he or she sees or hears something unusual.

This psychologist also mentioned similar to situations when someone threatens suicide, we need to tell someone and seek help. Being aware of what your friends or classmates say and taking things seriously can help. I told the class not to worry about tattling. Saving a life must rate higher than worries about hurt feelings.

One teen said he could not understand how something like this could happen in Colorado and the entire event made no sense to him. Several heads nodded in agreement.

After another long pause, the pastor spoke, "This week put us all in shock. Many times, in my life I did not understand the reason for some things, like this week. I cannot explain why this happened, but I believe we must rely on our faith. I do know faith in God can bring peace to all of us and this is what I want for you and everyone involved in this. We must continue to pray about this and maybe in time, we will understand more. I wish I could give you a better answer, but I encourage you to pray about this, talk with your friends and family, and remain faithful."

The pastor noted the end of the hour. He thanked everyone for coming and speaking up. We gathered in a big circle hug, for the closing prayer. The pastor offered a poignant prayer. He asked God for peace, comfort, and wisdom to deal with the events of the week. He asked God to remember the families of those killed and those who did the killings and urged all of us to think like Christ when dealing with tragedies like this. He closed the prayer with a request for guidance in the days ahead.

Author, far left, with class at Hope UMC

I told the pastor later his presence helped us, just by being in class that day. He smiled and said, "It comes with the job. In many ways, this is like meeting family members when someone dies. Merely being there can be comforting. I hope the teens rely on their faith and their loved ones to help them through this."

The Sunday after Columbine stands out in my memory. The pastor and the class made me proud of my association with the community of faith. God forbid I see again such a week in my life.

CHAPTER THIRTEEN

Paul Gets Stoned

As I developed one of the yearlong study topics the thought occurred to me one of the characters in the New Testament, other than Jesus, might make a great topic to pique the imagination of today's young Christians. I decided to focus on the idea of a hero.

I wanted to be clear heroes are heroes regardless of gender and because this came before gender neutrality I borrowed a word from Maya Angelou, shero, a female hero. The name itself caught some attention, and it gave me an interesting word to match the male oriented hero.

Who is the hero/shero of the New Testament? Jesus, of course. But as God's son, he did not fill the role of a human hero/shero. Who else comes to mind? Peter, Paul, Stephen, John, or perhaps, Mary Magdalene?

To begin, I asked about heroes they knew. I wanted the answers to come from them. They responded with the usual suspects;

celebrities and rock stars. Their ideas allowed us to expand the conversation to how they distinguished celebrities from heroes. This made the class dig a little deeper intellectually and come up with their ideas. Some of their responses follow.

"Celebrities are well known, they appear in the news all the time, but this doesn't make them heroes."

"Celebrities come from the press and publicity they receive, not necessarily for things they did."

"I think heroes must accomplish something good, like maybe, helping others."

"Heroes are people who made a difference in your life, you know, impacted your life in a positive way."

I added some classic definitions to these terms. A hero/shero is a mythological or legendary figure, often of divine descent endowed with great strength or ability (think Hercules), or, one admired for achievements and qualities, usually courage, righteousness, and fairness. A celebrity is a noted person; one honored or held up for public recognition and acclaim, one widely known to the general population.

In the fall of 1997, as we began the class, two events gave us great examples for this topic. We used Princess Diana and Mother Teresa as examples for celebrities and/or hero/sheroes.

Princess Diana died at age thirty-six on August 31, 1997, while one of the most famous and recognized people on the planet. A car accident, resulting from evasive tactics to escape publicity photographers, killed her. Millions viewed her funeral via television. Many held ideas of her as British royalty, a wife, a mother, and activist for various noble causes. She left two sons and an estate valued at approximately $35 million.

Within a week of Diana's death, Mother Teresa died at the age of eighty-seven. For forty-eight years, she served the poor, the outcast, and the sick people of a metropolitan area containing over 13.5 million people. Mother Teresa led a group of over 4,000 nuns operating orphanages, soup kitchens, homeless shelters, clinics, and schools. She professed human dignity for all people, regardless of situation or station, especially those deemed untouchable as the lowest caste of Indian society. She died with no possessions.

A year or so before this happened I talked with a member of the church and Janos' name came up. She asked if I kept in touch with him or knew his location. I responded I understood he remained in prison but admitted I did not keep in touch with him. Our conversation made me curious, so, the same afternoon, I went online, found his location, and contact information. I figured because I talked about him to the class for years I would reach out to him. To my great surprise, I got a quick response to my letter and we began a correspondence which continues today.

One of our exchanges touched on this hero/celebrity dichotomy and Janos shared some thoughts.

He wrote:

Take the either/or proposition of being a celebrity or a hero. I like the example of a sports writer covering the New York Yankees back when teams rode trains. One night a woman in a negligee comes running through the press car, screaming. Seconds later Babe Ruth comes in obviously drunk, and asking where the woman went. After a silent pause, one of the reporters said: "Well, it's a good thing none of us saw it." The story was not told until after Ruth retired.

They allowed him to remain a hero. Heroes, in my opinion, are supposed to be ideal people who we all aspire to be like—people so perfectly wonderful, even if you fall short of that goal, you have done well to try. The thing about heroes is they are mythic and myths must be allowed to survive.

Heroes are like Rorschach inkblot tests. What people see in their heroes says more about them than it does about the person they see as heroic. People have preconceived notions about what qualities are admirable and heroic, such as bravery, endurance, or strength. When they see a person who displays or represents one of those qualities, they make them their hero and bestow upon them the other qualities they consider heroic.

Heroes take action. Celebrities make gestures. It is like the difference between being nice and being kind. To me, being nice is just a polite, friendly, courteous way of treating others that makes you likable. Kindness is when you act nice and it somehow costs you something. Kindness involves making a sacrifice on a personal level.

The deaths of Mother Teresa and Princess Diana made me think celebrity and heroism were mutually exclusive. The press did not cover Mother Teresa half as much, even though she was a real saint. They covered Diana as the most tragic event in history. Mother Teresa didn't get as much adulation, but whom do you think parents would want their child to grow up to be like?

I believe heroes need to begin as idealized, mythic, larger than life examples. Then children can learn to identify them in a way that later in life allows those children to recognize heroic qualities in everyday people. Then, they learn to recognize the duality of humanity, and they can look 'behind' them and see some heroic quality. The quest to be heroic then shifts to trying to live up to the heroic quality.

Janos' letter added some reality to his persona. Many in the class doubted my story about Janos. Over the years, only two or three accused me of fabricating the entire story, but sharing this correspondence, and showing his photos, convinced even the most skeptical he exists.

I liked Janos' idea of heroes beginning as idealized, mythic, larger-than-life examples. I also liked the idea of seeing heroic qualities in everyday people and trying to follow their example. Other than Jesus, who in the New Testament fills this role?

When reading the New Testament, especially Acts of the Apostles, we find many examples of idealized, almost mythic, larger-than-life behavior. The book portrays how the early Christians, filled with the Holy Spirit—God's presence in each one of us—built communities that eventually grew into the modern church.

To me Saul, who later became Paul, jumps out as heroic. I decided to portray Paul this way to the class, especially the events after his confrontation by Christ. His life presents an action-filled adventure story if ever I saw one.

To lay the groundwork we spent a lesson or two discussing Paul's life, highlighted by the Greek culture dating back to Alexander the Great. Discussing an historical figure added to the reality and immediacy of Paul's life and the first century Christians. We overlaid this with the Roman culture, recently beginning its 400-year domination of the region. Because most knew King Herod and Pontius Pilate, the teens assumed the Roman culture dominated. The remaining strong influence of

Greek culture surprised the class. Jewish influence also complicated the secular cultures of the time.

Because many teens think history is boring, I needed to intersperse questions and tales of action into the presentations. I asked about the language of the New Testament. Hebrew, Latin, Spanish, Jewish, Christian, Romanian, and the code of Jerusalem—one of my favorites—came as answers to the question. Over the six or seven times we covered this in thirty-three years, no one offered Greek as the answer.

I remembered from an early age hearing one of my great aunts wanted to go to Baylor University and learn Greek so she could read the New Testament in its original language. She wanted to know what it *really* said—without translations.

Getting the class to understand why the original New Testament used Greek got us started. Most expressed surprise this tied to Alexander the Great since he brought Greek culture to the area three hundred years before Paul's time. Paul as a Roman citizen received certain privileges, so we also talked about the Roman influence. This included the concept of citizenship, respect for law and order, the roads built by the Romans, the relative peace across the empire, and their penchant for letter writing. We also added the Jewish influence, which included a love of the Law of Moses, knowledge of the Scriptures, a pervasive will to obey God, and the different factions: Pharisees, Sadducees, and Zealots.

We touched briefly on Saul of Tarsus as a Roman citizen, a Jew, a Pharisee, and as an educated man who wrote and read Greek. This helped the class understand the Pharisees considered the law as the most important thing and they held an unusual animosity toward the early Christians. This also set us up for an early action story: the stoning of Stephen found in Acts 7:58. It ends with the introduction of Saul: *"and the witnesses laid their coats at the feet of a young man named Saul."*

We discussed the brutality of stoning someone to death. Most knew the short story *The Lottery* by Shirley Jackson and jumped right in. This allowed us to tie Saul to such a brutal act and to discuss his motivations. I spent some time laying out the case for Saul as a villain. The scriptures portray him as vindictive, cruel, condescending, and overbearing. As a life-long Jew and a Pharisee, these Christians were anathema to everything he believed.

Saul's conversion is one of the most dramatic stories in Acts. The drama occurred as Saul headed to Damascus to arrest Christians and bring them back to Jerusalem for trial and possible death. As the story unfolds, Saul saw a light, heard the voice of Jesus/God, lost his sight, fell to the ground, requiring his fellow travelers to help him. With Saul in Damascus and still blind, God appeared to Ananias in a dream and told him to go and help Saul. One can imagine, given Saul's reputation, Ananias' reluctance.

I interrupted the story at the end of God's instructions to Ananias and said to the class, "God said to Ananias, go and help Saul and baptize him. What do you think Ananias said to God?" Best answer ever, came from a young woman who fully recognized the impact of what God asked. "You have *got* to be kidding," she added with enthusiasm. Right then, I felt good about being a Sunday school teacher. A lesson learned for everyone. Sometimes God asks us to do difficult things and our first answer might be "you've got to be kidding."

To top off Paul's life and to add more action, we worked out a lesson I called; Paul gets stoned. The wording gathered attention and interest, especially after Colorado passed a referendum allowing possession and use of moderate amounts of marijuana. The kids laughed and acted out smoking a joint when I announced the title.

Acts tells Paul's story of traveling to Lystra, performing miracles, and the people identified him as one of the Greek gods. Acts 14:11–20. We set the scene as though a television reporter came to interview Paul. I copied the famous line from the movie *Blues Brothers* "We are on a mission from God." The dialogue for the TV reporter and Paul went like this.

> **TV Reporter:** *Paul, the people at Lystra love you. They are calling you Mercury, and call Barnabas Jupiter. What do you think?*
>
> **Paul:** *They are confused. I am on a mission from God. Ever since I saw Jesus on the road to Damascus, I want everyone to know Jesus is the answer.*
>
> **TV Reporter:** *I hear some people are not happy with you. What do you think about the threats against you and Barnabas?*
>
> **Paul:** *I do not care. I am on a mission from God to tell everyone about Jesus.*

To get everyone involved, I wadded up newspaper sheets into loosely wrapped balls, held by masking tape. I put them in a big shopping bag. I kept the bag behind a chair until ready for use and then handed out three or four paper 'stones' to each one in the class. We got someone to volunteer to play Paul. At the appropriate time, everyone cut loose with the paper stones and blasted our Paul. Lots of energy, and paper stones, flying around the room!

On one such occasion, a woman agreed to be Paul and came up to recite her lines and get stoned. Her younger brother in the audience, took the opportunity to throw the paper stones, but also hurled his shoe at her. She sprang into action, came across the room, put him in a headlock, and started pummeling him. After thirty seconds or so, he gave in and she released him. I, along with the rest of the class, nearly drowned in laughter.

After the stoning, we resumed the interview:

TV Reporter: *Paul, how does it feel to be stoned? Weren't you afraid?*

Paul: *Of course, but Jesus told me to take the Good News to everyone.*

TV Reporter: *Why did the crowd stone you?*

Paul: *I challenged the way they think. They should not worship false gods. They need faith and to be baptized!*

TV Reporter: *After this stoning, are you going to quit talking about Jesus? Those people tried to kill you.*

Paul: *No! I told you I am on a mission from God. I must tell everyone about Jesus. I will travel to other places and tell people about Jesus.*

TV Reporter: *Well, thanks Paul. And, good luck. I think you will need it.*

We continued our story with Paul visiting Athens, Corinth, and Ephesus.

CHAPTER FOURTEEN

Sacred Sluts

How do you give a class a sense of geography, time, and place? I found maps and photos work well for this.

I love looking at maps and photos of locations I want to visit. During my high school years, I got a huge map of the United States, framed it and placed it in my room at home. I placed pushpins into the map for each place I traveled.

At first, the pins only showed Lubbock and Amarillo in Texas, and Ruidoso, New Mexico. Later I traveled with the Boy Scouts to the 1964 National Jamboree in Valley Forge, Pennsylvania. We came through Virginia, Tennessee, and Arkansas on our way home. Later through the benefits of a job requiring me to travel each week and the accompanying perquisite of frequent flyer miles, I traveled the world more than I ever imagined as a young boy.

Athens and Corinth, Greece, topped the list of my early travels. On the anniversary of my dad's death and frankly, to escape some of the sadness related to the date, I headed to

Greece in December 1990. As it happened, one of my former students spent her junior year of college in Athens the same year. She and her exchange student friends took me on a tour of the Acropolis, the Plaka, and the national museums.

I also loved taking photographs and collected thousands of slides and now, in recent years, thousands of digital photos of my travels. This combination allowed me to have pictures of some of the places Paul lived, preached, and developed Christian communities in the first century.

This gave me a great segue from Bible study to talk about plans for the high schoolers in class. It also opened many eyes to the possibilities awaiting them as they went to college. The photos also gave me great talking points.

As we studied Paul's travels to Athens, we talked about everyone having doubts at one time or another, even about things previously comfortable to their thinking. Acts of the Apostles relates Paul's genius and the human nature of doubts exhibited by the Greeks.

Athens, the storied city of history, culture, philosophy, government, and art, no wonder Paul wanted to go there. What a place for Paul to bring the story of Christ. Athens, the city of Socrates, Aristotle, and Plato provided a center of learned people for Paul. The Greeks worshiped many gods. The city contained many temples, some to this god, and others to other gods, and still others to gods who disappeared over the ages. Given this rich, historical background, Paul found a way to touch the lives of the learned men of Athens.

Paul went to the Areopagus, or the hill of Ares or Mars, depending on whose god you followed, the Greeks or the Romans. There he encountered the learned men of Athens, the Council of the Areopagus. The Council discussed the issues of the day, religion, and philosophy. It ruled over all matters pertaining to the religious life of Athens. When time came for Paul to speak, he took a different tack from his typical teaching. He made a different kind of speech, one departing from his usual style. The speech contained elements only found in one passage. He also employed contact points for his sophisticated listener's way of thinking.

Imagine Paul's reaction to seeing all the treasuries, monuments, statues, temples, and shrines to various gods. Paul knew well the first commandment of the ten passed to Moses: "You shall have no gods before me." He must have reacted deeply to the blatant blasphemy he saw throughout the city. Knowing this, one can imagine how Paul might unload on the Athenians, blasting them for their wicked ways. Instead, he eschewed the Jewish history lessons and instead talked about the story of Christ's crucifixion and resurrection.

Paul told the noblemen of Athens about walking around their fair city and seeing many temples to the various gods. Then he focused on the temple to the "unknown god," the catchall temple they used to cover all the bases. He tells them he is there to testify about the ever-living God, and even they, with all their tradition and history, made allowance for this god. Paul pointed out their doubts they covered all gods. Even with so many gods for so many different concepts, they wanted a catchall god, just in case.

The story gave us an opportunity to discuss doubt, a universal human trait. Regardless of your reading, study, and experience, times will come in your life when you have doubts. Doubts about yourself, your capabilities, your knowledge, and your concept of the world you live in. All of us have doubts and this is not a recent development. Paul used the doubts of the men of Athens to convince some the ever-living god is present and Paul is his representative.

Showing photos of the Areopagus where Paul stood to make these arguments added a personal touch to this story and gave it more than a storybook flavor. Many in the class wanted to know what people did on the Areopagus today. I told them, "Take pictures, and talk about the unknown god." Many of the tourists, including me, took photos, but I did not hear anyone talking about an unknown god.

The Areopagus sits below the Acropolis and provides stunning views of the ruins, including the Parthenon. Those photos of Emily and me on the same spot reported in Acts 34, gave the class a contemporary view of this location in Paul's travels. It also conveyed the timelessness of Paul's message.

We next talked about Paul's apparent confidence to join the noblemen of Athens in debate. Paul, a learned man in his own right, showed great courage by going into the midst of foreigners, strangers to him, and people with different attitudes about religion. The Holy Spirit surely accompanied Paul as he undertook this task on the Areopagus. Paul's experience in Athens served as a teaching moment of a hero nearly 2,000 years later.

Emily's role in my story and photos also conveyed a sense of possibility to the class. Several teens talked about where they might travel, if they could spend a college year abroad. Seeing her and the photos caught their attention. I trust the message about doubts, confidence, and the power of the Holy Spirit, gave them the idea they, too, could be heroes.

Modern Corinth lies about forty miles west of Athens. The new city existed only 100 years when Paul came in 51 CE, but boasted a population five times the size of Athens. Ancient Corinth, the original city founded in the tenth century BCE, grew into the richest port and largest city in ancient Greece. Its location, near two ports, one on the western side facing the Gulf of Corinth, and one on the eastern side, facing the Saronic Gulf added strategic importance. It led the Achaean League against the Romans in 146 BCE and the Legions levelled the city. For the next 100 years, the city hosted only squatters and transients. Julius Caesar re-founded the city as a colony in 44 BCE and it soon thrived. Paul visited this new Corinth to establish a vital Christian community.

We talked about why Paul would decide to settle in Corinth. Hosting a wide variety of people from around the eastern Mediterranean, New Corinth provided a young, active, growing population for Paul's ministry. The dynamic city gave many people the chance to shed their past lives and gain social acceptance and wealth. Paul appeared unintimidated by a bustling, cosmopolitan city, perhaps because no dominant religious or intellectual tradition dominated. The city may have reminded Paul of his hometown of Tarsus or of Syrian Antioch, the city of his home church or community.

However, in many respects the new city could not escape the reputation of the ancient one. This gave me a new catch phrase to garner attention and curiosity from the class. This also provided a springboard for discussion of perhaps Paul's most famous writing, the essay on Love from First Corinthians, Chapter 13. The catch phrase: The sacred sluts of Corinth.

Ancient historians reported 1,000 sacred prostitutes in the Temple of Aphrodite located on the Acrocorinth, a hill overlooking the city from the south. In addition, one of the Greek slang words for fornication derived from the city's name, making the ancient view of the city as an especially licentious place, hard to shake.

Sacred prostitutes, now there is a term to catch the ear of teenage boys. First, they could not believe the Sunday school teacher said the words, and second, how could he tie this into a lesson on Jesus, Paul as a hero, or anything else? I started with oxymoron, the linking of two contradictory or incongruous words into one phrase. Most sophomores and juniors studied the vocabulary words in preparation for the SAT or ACT tests. These tests gave a common experience to many in the class and made them familiar with the word.

The class lit up, often saying, "Oh, yeah, we know this. Cruel kindness, military intelligence, loving hate, or jumbo shrimp."

I continued, "Sacred—set apart for the service or worship of deity, entitled to reverence, holy. And, Slut—a lewd woman or prostitute."

This discussion acknowledged their common experience of college preparation and encouraged them to apply their knowledge to new areas. Sacred sluts contained a ribald quality to let them think they were discussing an adult topic or getting away with something. Either way, I engaged them.

Many knew Aphrodite as the goddess of love, but most did not think in carnal terms. Okay, the boys probably did think in those terms, but love and beauty were general terms teens thought about and admired. This gave me an entry to discuss fertility, sexual relations, and all aspects of love, from the noble end of the spectrum to the raunchiest.

Some expressed shock the Corinthian girls, or sacred sluts, populated the temple and accommodated the worshipers, after receiving a fee, of course. The entire class easily identified this practice as prostitution and found it difficult getting their minds around such a practice as a religious experience.

The concept of love, exhibited by the cult of Aphrodite in ancient times, gave us a convenient intro to Paul's paean to love.

Since this part of Paul's writing comes at weddings, and sometimes funerals, the class showed a passing familiarity to it. Most, however, never studied or conducted an exegesis of this scripture.

We spent a session talking about the Greek terms for love: philia, storge, eros, and agape. Many knew Philadelphia as the City of Brotherly Love but did not know it came from one of the Greek words, so we discussed brotherly love—love for humankind or others, as a brother. Storge, a second word for love, referred to family love, the kind between a parent and child. Eros, love directed toward physical pleasure, lust, sex—this term most teenage boys knew but lacked knowledge of its Greek origin. Agape, the love to transcend human sex drive, physical or familial terms. A divine love or the ultimate love God has for us.

Some called this writing of Paul's The New Testament Psalm of Love and compared it to the forty-fifth Psalm and the Song of Solomon from the Old Testament. It deserves a close reading but may lose some of its power and beauty if one over-analyzes it. Reading through the passages with a group of high school aged young folks can be a joy and a revelation.

Paul begins by telling the Corinthians love is superior to all gifts. Some background on spiritual gifts like speaking in tongues and prophecy, and their meaning to the first century Christians in Corinth, laid the groundwork. Next Paul lists things one can do—have knowledge, show faith, bestow goods on the poor, give your body to be burned, or suffer long, but if these are not done with the spirit of love, they fall short.

Next, Paul describes love and its antithesis. It is longsuffering and kind. It is *not* envious, proud, arrogant, rude, nor does it seek its own interests, is not provoked, thinks no evil, and does not rejoice in iniquity. Next Paul expands on what love is—strong, believing, hopeful, and enduring. He continues about the permanence of love—it never fails. Then he illustrates the temporary nature of the gifts of prophecy and speaking in tongues and contrasts these with the permanence of love. He sums up with "and now abide faith, hope, love, these three, but the greatest of these is love."

As we discussed the examination of these verses and in response to my question of what do you think of the Paul's summation, one of the students said, "It is obvious to me. Of course, love is the greatest. When we spend eternity with God, we will not need faith or hope. God knows everything and is eternal, what does he need with faith or hope? But God *is* love and will always be love."

The young man became an associate pastor of a large Presbyterian Church, on the A list for certain. Although I led the class, in this case, he taught me.

View of the Acropolis, Athens, Greece from the Areopagus

CHAPTER FIFTEEN

The Eighty-Nine-Year-Old Visitor

One Sunday an elderly lady, at least in her eighties, smiling from ear to ear, stuck her head in the door of our classroom. She exuded a warm and inviting demeanor that welcomed conversation.

"What class is this?" She stuck her head in the door and looked around.

Glancing at her and assuming she did not want the high school class, I used my lawyer tactic of answering a question with another question, "What class are you looking for?"

Most of the adult classes were at the other end of the building down a winding corridor. I thought we could send someone with her to avoid more time lost while she tried to find her class at the other end of the church. The elderly woman about five-foot three inches tall and maybe 100 pounds answered, "The Senior High class." Her gleaming eyes and bright ear-to-ear smile continued to radiate through the doorway.

I heard only the senior part of her sentence and said, "Oh, this is the senior high class, not one for seniors." I thought she might be ninety-years old and I should speak slower and more clearly.

"Yes, that is the one I seek. The senior high class. May I join?"

Knowing I could not refuse, but still a little confused, I asked more, "Are you sure?"

"Yes, quite sure. May I?" She walked in and looked for a seat before I could think of anything else to say.

Since the teens sat anywhere from a bean bag, to a bungie-cord chair, to a dilapidated couch, to the floor, I scrambled to find her a real chair, one appropriate for someone her age. Surely, she made a mistake. Why would she want to be in *this* class?

When I mentioned earlier the class covered youth, I overlooked the fact young people come in all ages. At the age of

Helen Gail Mangold

eighty-nine, Helen Gail Mangold walked into our class and made as much, if not more, contribution as any of us. Young at heart described her best. She enjoyed relating to younger folks, both the teens and me.

Helen Gail, she eschewed just Helen, outlived three husbands, and lived an extraordinary life. She revealed a quick-wit, a gregarious, even charismatic nature, and a well-rounded education. She lived in a retirement home near the church and inquired about classes for young people with several older members who lived in the same place. One of the founding members of the church mentioned off-handedly I led a class for the high school kids. She and an elderly neighbor, who drove them to church, seldom attended the early service, but came in time for classes and fellowship time between the services. Helen Gail announced she would like to attend the high school class and asked if she could do that.

The way I heard the story, the charter member told her she should do whatever she wanted, and Helen Gail made plans accordingly.

Typically, the oldest in our class, I loved it when other adults joined us from time to time. One father came to class for three years. He merely showed up at the appointed time. He did not add much to class, but observed the kids, our topics, and me. With his son in the class, my paranoia ran rampant, imagining a dossier on my teaching skills for the Youth Ministries staff. The result? A report undoubtedly calling for my immediate removal as teacher.

After a few weeks, I decided he held a genuine interest, not one of reporting on me. He later praised the rapport we enjoyed in class and spoke well of our topics and discussions. His son asked me for a recommendation to support his nomination to Eagle Scout and later asked me to speak at his Honor Court where he received his award. The father, his son, and I remain friends twenty years after they attended the class.

Working on the idea of keeping teens interested in learning something about Christianity, I became a bit flustered the first weeks Helen Gail sat with us. I feared something I said would upset her or go contrary to her beliefs. I became cautious and more circumspect about saying whatever came to mind. Turned out Helen Gail, remarkably attuned to the younger generation, sparkled with humor. Her family contained grandchildren in their early thirties and other relatives in their teens and she continually communicated with them.

My wife and I took Helen Gail to dinner a couple of times. Because older folks do not usually drive at night, and look for the senior specials, we drove and picked her up around 5:00 p.m. Delightful, talkative, attentive, and a great listener, she made a great dinner partner. She jumped into topics she knew something about and we enjoyed a wide-ranging conversation.

We learned she lived in Turkey with one of her husbands, an agronomist with the U.S. government Agency for International Development. Living in the region where Paul established many of the early Christian communities, she knew the current culture, history, topography, and geography of the area. I told her the class studied Paul as a Hero every fourth year and he would be next year's topic.

When we came to Paul's experience in Ephesus, on the western edge of modern Turkey, Helen Gail added to the conversation. She visited the site and knew how the ancient city looked today. She shared some photographs, forty-year-old Kodachrome slides, taken in the 1960s. I visited Ephesus in 1998, also taking many photos. We compared photos and found many covered the same sites. We showed many to the class to their great enjoyment.

An extremely wealthy city during Paul's time Ephesus served as an entry port to Asia Minor and points east in the Roman Empire. Already 1,000 years old when Paul visited in 52 CE, its history included the Persians, Alexander the Great, and the

Romans. They controlled the area from 133 BCE and at the time of Paul's stay there.

Choosing Ephesus as a base made sense to Paul because of its large, cosmopolitan population. Being a religious center, home to many cultures, as well as a political and economic center, it served Paul well. The city hosted many different ethnic groups along with their ideas of worship, magic, and miracles. For centuries, one of the Seven Wonders of the Ancient World called Ephesus home. I used this fact to open a class discussion on these wonders and to provide a teaching link to Paul's work.

Most could identity the Pyramids of Egypt as one of the seven wonders, and the only one still standing, but few knew the others. As we talked about them, some of the class would join in, suddenly remembering something they read, heard, or saw on an obscure television show.

I gave out hints to keep the conversation flowing. King Mausolus of Caria led to "Oh, yeah, the Mausoleum!" and The Lighthouse on the island of Pharos led to "The Lighthouse at Alexandria!" and less often, Nebuchadnezzar built and irrigated these . . . "Hanging Gardens of Babylon!" They often remembered more as the discussion progressed and certainly knew more than I did at the same age.

The others? The Statue of Zeus (Jupiter) at Olympia, the Colossus of Rhodes, and the Temple of Artemis (Diana), at Ephesus. Four times the size of the Parthenon in Athens, the Temple of Artemis measured seventy-five yards wide and one-hundred-forty yards long. Its 127 columns towered six and a half stories above the base and reached six feet in diameter. The temple presented an impressive and overwhelming sight to ancient travelers.

Acts, Chapter 19 relates one of Paul's famous disputes with the people of Ephesus. He railed against the worship of Artemis and dismissed the centuries old practices related to the temple. He blasted those who owned small figurines of Artemis: worshipers, travelers, and pilgrims, and derided those who kept the statues in honored places in their homes. Paul's success in converting many to Christ and his constant preaching against Artemis led to an upheaval by the silversmiths who made a living producing the figurines for sale. Paul's actions threatened their livelihood and they determined to take action.

The mob grew and became threatening to Paul. Even though Ephesus welcomed most of the pantheon of gods, Artemis, the patron goddess of Ephesus became the focus for those opposing Paul. The theater or arena in Ephesus held 25,000 and the mob gathered there to protest Paul's teachings. Supporters warned Paul not to go near the theater for fear of his life. We do not know if Paul ever preached in the theater for the only reference to Paul and the theater is the warning not to go into the theater to preach. Acts 19:30

One of the highlights of a tour of modern-day Ephesus includes the remains of the theater. It lies near the end of the ancient city and overlooks the Harbor Street. In Paul's day, the end of Harbor Street met the water and hosted a bustling port. In the two thousand years since, the harbor silted up and the water, while still visible, lies far in the distance.

Both Helen Gail and I had photos of us standing on the stage or presentation area of the theater. We converted Helen Gail's old Kodachrome slide into a digital format and juxtaposed it with my photo taken in 1998. Comparing the photos showed the efforts to restore the theater to its original look. The

Helen Gail Mangold at the theater in Ephesus, circa 1967, author in the same location 1998

class loved the photos and asked Helen Gail many questions about Ephesus and her time in Turkey. This seemed to please her and I certainly enjoyed having her add to the substance of our studies.

While in Ephesus, I purchased a souvenir statue of Artemis. My wife chided me for going against Paul's teachings. My purchase appeared to violate Paul's admonition. Made of plastic, not silver, it only cost a few dollars, but it clearly represented the goddess Artemis/Diana. Thinking quickly, I defended myself by declaring it for instructional purposes only. I would use the souvenir as a prop during our study of Paul's time in Ephesus.

Helen Gail attended our class for three years before her health began to fail. Those years included some of the best times for the class and her presence added a modicum of seriousness to our studies. Having the teens see an elderly woman attend regularly, participate in our discussion, and add immensely to the quality of the experience gave us a Holy Spirit experience none of us anticipated.

Sometime later, a class member, Dani Rowland, got the opportunity to give back to Helen Gail. One of the high schools where many of our students attended took their choir to the retirement home where Helen Gail lived. Many of the residents, Helen Gail thought as many as two hundred, attended the choir performance.

Dani sang in this choir. As the crowd settled in and the choir took their places on the risers, Dani walked down from the stage and into the audience, delaying the performance. Helen Gail's poor eyesight prevented her from seeing who came into the audience. Being the target never entered her mind as Dani went up the aisle, stopped right in front of Helen Gail and gave her a big hug.

Of course, when she got close, Helen Gail recognized Dani and beamed at the hug and the attention. Many of the choir members assumed a relationship of grandmother-granddaughter, or even great grandmother-great granddaughter between Helen Gail and Dani and murmured about it until they learned they attended the same Sunday school class. Helen Gail could not wait to tell me. She called me that night to brag on Dani and told me her co-residents considered her the celebrity of the day because of Dani's actions before the choir performance. This act of kindness between classmates made Helen Gail's day. Her neighbors loved the whole thing and talked about it for weeks.

Upon deciding to lead a Sunday school class for teens, I never expected to set up bonding moments between people with seventy years or more between them. Spending a year talking about Paul as a Hero allowed us one year to discover two other sheroes, Helen Gail Mangold and Dani Rowland. Both go on the accomplished list.

CHAPTER SIXTEEN

Why Lord?

"Did you hear about Carei? I can't believe it." He blurted into the phone.

"Hear what? I haven't heard anything." My mind raced, wondering what to think. Carei Coughlin, a beautiful, outgoing, and charismatic teen, attended our class. Seventeen years old, Carei showed maturity beyond her years. She knew what she wanted and feared nothing. I wondered whether she did something on a dare and it turned sour.

As evidence for her strong-minded nature, she recently decided to change her name. She decided to change her birth name *Carrie*, because she decided Carei carried more cachet. In class, she often spoke up before the others and held strong opinions. Whatever happened, I hoped she had not broken any bones.

"She died last night. Some kind of seizure or something. She's gone."

Because of being around machine gun fire during my Marine training, I don't hear well and that morning, my hearing aids lay on the counter. "What did you say? I thought you said she died."

"That's right. It's unbelievable. So young and full of life." We quickly ended our phone conversation. The caller gave no hard information about what happened. Stunned, I sat back in a chair thinking.

By this time, Carei's older sister graduated high school, but Carei and her younger brother were class members. If it only happened the night before many of the class may not yet know the news. By Sunday morning, I knew the local grapevine would provide the news to most everyone.

This happened right before Christmas in 1997, thirteen years after I started working with the teens and just as I felt some confidence about my role for the class. Her death challenged and jolted me along with our community of faith. I received the call on Saturday morning December 20th.

I began to think about how I could discuss this with the class the next morning. My planned Christmas theme for the last Sunday prior to the holiday flew out the window. I needed to regroup. Several calls on Saturday confirmed the terrible news. How does one talk teenagers through such a shocking loss? I experienced the death of my father, but not a shocking event like this. His death came after illness and some time to digest the possibility of his death. But with this sudden death, what could I say to the class?

Our class on Sunday experienced no joy of the Christmas season. The teens were shocked and in a state of disbelief. We talked about Carei and told things we remembered about her. I tried to focus the class on positive or funny things we remembered about her, but the black cloud of despair hung over us that day. We knew few details about her death but knew its reality. Many wondered how this could happen. Some asked the ultimate faith question. Why?

I reminded the class we belong to a community of faith and this can be a source of consolation. We had each other to walk with us as we made this difficult journey through grief. Could they focus on how they could support Carei's family with tenderness and grace? Maybe they could help with practical items—shopping, running errands, etc. Or, maybe, come as a friend and listen. I felt inadequate to counsel them, partly because of my state of denial. Surely, this did not happen.

The main sanctuary hosted Carei's funeral the day before Christmas Eve. Everyone appeared shocked, but somehow, we made it through the service. Carei's wishes were for cremation with scattering of ashes in the Rocky Mountains near Breckenridge where she loved to go with her family. Those wishes gave another example of her mature nature and foresight.

Carei loved the poem *I'm Spending Christmas with Jesus This Year*. The bulletin for her service included a copy with a notation from her: Thank you for holding and loving my family. Carei Ann.

A portion of the poem follows.

> *I can't tell you of the splendor, or the peace here in this place.*
>
> *Can you just imagine Christmas with our Savior face to face?*
>
> *I'll ask him to light your spirit, as I tell him of your love.*
>
> *So then pray one for another as you lift your eyes above.*

So please let your hearts be joyful, and let your spirit sing.
For I'm spending Christmas in Heaven and I'm walking with the King.

How ironic to read those words at Carei's service right before Christmas. The next day lacked any joy associated with seeing past class members at Christmas Eve services.

Can we see good things resulting from terrible losses? Yes, but such vision takes time.

Linda Coughlin Brooks, Carei's mother, worked as a registered nurse at the time of Carei's death. Linda found her unconscious. Reacting with her professional training, Linda worked feverishly trying to revive Carei while calling 911. Linda related later how it became a blessing of sorts because if others had found Carei and worked to revive her, Linda would always doubt their efforts and wonder whether they tried everything to save her life. Knowing she did everything she could to save Carei gave her some comfort.

This loss became a crossroads for Linda. Linda took her professional training and her curiosity as a mom and explored all details of what happened to Carei. Linda's efforts were groundbreaking in the diagnosis of SUDEP (Sudden Unexpected Death in Epilepsy) for Carei's death. This is a fatal complication of epilepsy defined as the sudden and unexpected, non-traumatic death of a person with epilepsy coupled with no toxicological or anatomical cause of death.

Linda worked with the local coroner to undertake a review of hundreds of sudden deaths in the area with undetermined causes. The review caused many cases to change the cause of death to SUDEP. The study also resulted in new training for coroners that raised awareness of SUDEP.

Linda did not stop there. She worked extensively with the Epilepsy Foundation and developed a grief counseling process to assist loved ones who experience SUDEP and other losses. She took an active role in Partners Against Mortality in Epilepsy (PAME) where medical professionals and families share their stories and raise awareness about the risks associated with epilepsy, especially SUDEP. Linda's efforts touched the lives of thousands of people because, I believe, of the path she took after Carei's death. While nothing replaces Carei, many later benefited from Linda's determination and actions.

Carei and Linda's story touched a personal note with me. My mother lived a wonderful, active life until she died at age 92. However, she buried three of her daughters, my sisters. She remarked more than once this violated the natural order of things. Children should bury parents, not the other way around, yet she remained an optimistic and hopeful person all the remaining years of her life.

Occurrences such as these cause faithful people to ask if God is all-powerful and wants the best for his people, why and how can there be suffering in the world? I don't know a good answer for this, but I have seen how good things can result from our suffering.

Belonging to any community of faith for thirty-three years naturally brings change and loss. Our Sunday school class proved no different. Over this period, we lost several classmates, parents, siblings, friends, and acquaintances. Dealing with deaths in general is hard enough, but the loss of teenagers can be devastating, for families, loved ones, friends, and classmates. Our class experienced the chaos and disorientation that often accompanies these deaths. Loss by suicide is particularly difficult.

Suicides for teens represent about eleven percent of teenage deaths. Unfortunately, the number is growing. Today's teens face excruciating anxiety over any number of influences and events and suicide can appear as a solution.

Our class experienced this on more than one occasion. Because our society looks for cause and effect, many assume dysfunction with the family or parents of these teens. The result is often little or no discussion about the suicide, especially between adults and teens. Maybe we fear putting ideas into the heads of young people or this societal shaming puts a lid on free discussion. Whatever the reasons, we do a poor job in my judgment, about talking through the issues of teen suicide.

When confronted by teens in our class about reasons for teen suicide, I attempted to create a safe environment for discussion. The lawyer training I received often led me to turn the tables by asking, "What do you think?" Sometimes this worked and other times the class clammed up and looked to me for guidance.

I knew some teen suicides result from feelings of hopelessness and helplessness and I asked the class about it. Often because teens have less experience in life, they see no solution to their situation. Sometimes they see death as a way out.

Other situations come from trying to escape feelings of pain, rejection, hurt or being unloved. Sometimes they come from loss or feeling victimized by others. They may feel such feelings are unbearable and will never end. Thus, thoughts of escaping by suicide.

During these conversations, I reverted to things we believed. I reminded the class everyone is worthy of love and respect. God loves us and others love us, even if we cannot feel it at a particular time. A community of faith such as ours can lend support during these tough times. While such answers may help those contemplating suicide, they are of little solace to parents or loved ones suffering a loss to suicide. Things do change however, with time.

I hoped a personal witness about my experience after losing my father, my mother and three sisters could help talk about these losses. I told of the intense pain and grief that comes immediately after a death. I tried to convey my belief, built upon my experience, things do improve and time provides a way of ameliorating the grief. The grief never goes completely away, but it becomes tolerable. I reminded the class how, after a while, we tend to remember good times and asked them to focus on such when thinking of lost loved ones.

I used our closing prayer time to urge us all to have the courage and strength to reach out to those experiencing grief. I believed the adage of strength in numbers and encouraged empathy and love to others.

I saw an example of this community strength when we experienced another devastating loss. Years later, at the age of fifteen, a classmate received a diagnosis of non-Hodgkin's lymphoma, a rarity for children and youth. The high school group knew her well because her two older sisters participated in class and the youth group.

One Sunday after she became sick and during chemotherapy and radiation treatments, she came to class. She lost all her hair and like many teens experienced anxiety about her appearance. Actually, saying she came to class is wrong. Her sisters brought her.

Their attendance surprised me, but I determined to have a regular day in class. I welcomed them and told Courtney and Kari it pleased me to see them and Jenna. I made a joke about despite them graduating the class; they missed class so much they must be back for a refresher. I directed my attention to the older girls, not wanting to focus on Jenna.

Courtney and Kari smiled and took their seats. Jenna responded with a half-smile, but I sensed a gladness for no one making a big deal out of her presence or showing nervousness about her appearance. As a bright light who loved music and showed a wicked sense of humor, Jenna boosted many by her presence even during the dark days of chemotherapy and radiation. It felt good to have her in class again.

We proceeded with the lesson and Courtney and Kari made some comments about Charlie saying the same things three and five years ago when they were in class. I acted outraged and defensive and made some remark about when things are perfect, you don't need to change. The give and take seemed to break any tension and soon we were laughing and kidding each other. Jenna even jumped in with some zingers. I don't remember the particular lesson, but the hour flew by. It was a good morning.

Before long, Jenna's condition worsened, and we all feared for her. On June 5, 2008, Jenna Katherine Anderson died at age sixteen. Our hearts ached for her suffering and then her death. Hope church held her funeral service on a beautiful summer evening and young people packed the sanctuary. They came from Jenna's school, her hometown, and from our youth group. It pleased me so many turned out to show their love and affection for Jenna.

A volunteer choir teeming with teens and young adults sang "Seasons of Love" from the Broadway hit *Rent*. They sang out with strength and verve. The singing rang from the rafters.

Five hundred twenty-five thousand six hundred minutes.
Five hundred twenty-five thousand journeys to plan.
Five hundred twenty-five thousand six hundred minutes.
How do you measure a life of a woman or a man?
In truths that she learned,
Or in times that he cried?
In bridges he burned,
or the way that she died?
It's time now to sing out,
though the story never ends.
Let's celebrate, remember a year in a life
of friends.

During the service, I remembered the Sunday Courtney and Kari brought Jenna to our class. Recalling the fun times and the joy our community of faith provided that day warmed my heart. On that occasion, Jenna took her place as one of many, no special attention. I think she loved it. We still rejoice in our memories of her.

Such times can create a crisis of faith, especially in young people trying to figure out how to deal with the world. Anger and resentment often flare in their minds. The same questions always arise: How can God let this happen? And, why does God allow suffering and then death, especially for young people?

Many faithful Christians have the same thoughts and questions. This does not detract from the love and support that comes from belonging to a community of faith, like a Sunday school class or a church family. Through my comments to youth,

I sought to give them tools they can use when something terrible happens. I also stressed things will improve with time and we can often look back and see positive things resulting from such losses.

The lost loved ones, the sisters caring for each other, the mom going to great lengths to raise awareness of SUDEP, and our small community of faith, all go on the A list.

Name Plaques in Hope UMC's Memorial Garden

CHAPTER SEVENTEEN

Easter Goes to Court

Each spring, the most important date in the church calendar arrives, bringing new outfits, lilies, and great attendance for worship services. Easter offers hope and inspiration to Christians everywhere. Given this importance, our class delved into the mystery of Easter during the weeks preceding it each year.

One signal tenet separates Christianity from other religions of the world—the resurrection of Jesus. The living Jesus endures in the faith and witness of all Christians.

Other religions typically know their leaders/saviors/prophets and follow their teachings, but they do not claim such leaders/saviors/prophets live today. Christians serve a resurrected Lord, one who overcame not only physical death, but the power and fear of death. They do not simply preach a creed or philosophy but claim to know personally the living Jesus and vow to follow him.

On several occasions in the weeks leading up to Easter Sunday, I queried the class about their beliefs on the resurrection of Jesus. For conservative or fundamental Christians, the results were disheartening. The class invariably voted only one-third to forty percent as believing the physical resurrection of Jesus as an historical fact. The majority did not believe it or asked for an undecided designation. Digging deeper into their thoughts revealed the scientific methods taught in schools created much skepticism of this miracle.

They agreed memory or ethics of Jesus could live in your heart but doubted the physical process through which he came back to life. The physics necessary for such an event escaped them. Reconciling this mystery in their minds often presented a concept too far.

One young woman indicated the idea struck her more as a myth or legend but agreed with the teachings of Jesus. Her logical, oriented-to-the-scientific-method brain could not wrap around this issue. I asked her to think more about the idea and look at the evidence to support this radical idea.

One reference we reviewed came from an unlikely source, a Jewish scholar, Hugh Schonfield. In his book *The Passover Plot*, the non-practicing Jewish author who spoke Greek, Latin, Hebrew, Aramaic, and English, surmised Jesus plotted to take a soporific and pretend to die. This would create an uprising among the people and then he would awaken and lead them. The plot went wrong when soldiers thrust a lance into his side and Jesus died. Schonfield pays tribute to the power of the resurrection, if not as fact, but certainly as evidence of a living savior in the hearts of followers.

His quote, from *The Passover Plot*, 1965, Element Books:

"The Messianic program was saved from the grave of all dead hopes to become a guiding light and inspiration to men. Whenever mankind strives to bring in the rule of justice, righteousness and peace, there the deathless presence of Jesus the Messiah is with them. Whenever a people of God is found laboring in the cause of human brotherhood, love and compassion, there the King of the Jews is enthroned. No other will ever come to be what he was and do what he did."

Watching trials in my father's courtroom, talking with the court reporters and attorneys, and understanding how evidence works in court, gave me a lawyer's idea about teaching this basic Christian belief to the class. I felt equipped to do this. I received an American Jurisprudence Award for the highest grade in my Evidence class at law school. Over my career, I witnessed and participated in many court trials before landing the Sunday school teaching job. How could I build a case for the resurrection of Jesus?

Scientific methods require repeatable laboratory results to prove a premise or proposition. There is no way to repeat the resurrection of Jesus. Many Christians believe the resurrection as an historical fact, but only a onetime event. Therefore, we must look elsewhere for proof. This involved the legal-historical method, as in, the same way courts receive evidence to prove guilt or innocence, establish a premise, or persuade the court or jury of a fact or proposition.

Lawyers understand the most important piece of evidence is not a murder weapon, blood tests, forensic debris, or a physical object, but testimony from witnesses. Most trials turn on what someone said from the witness stand. This gave me an idea of presenting a case for the resurrection of Jesus as though the class stood in the place of judge or jury. Luckily, the Bible provides plenty of witnesses to the resurrection story.

Law school and my experience served me well in this instance. I thought of these Biblical witnesses and came up with evidence to lay before the class.

First, I talked about Jesus' own predictions of his death and resurrection. The gospel of Mark says, *"As they were coming down the mountain, Jesus gave them orders not to tell anyone what they had seen until the Son of Man had risen from the dead. They kept the matter to themselves, discussing what 'rising from the dead' meant." Mark 9:9-10*

John's gospel adds, *"Jesus answered them, 'Destroy this temple, and I will raise it again in three days.' The Jews replied, 'It has taken forty-six years to build this temple, and you are going to raise it in three days?' But the temple he had spoken of was his body. After he was raised from the dead, his disciples recalled what he had said. Then they believed the scripture and the words that Jesus had spoken." John 2:19-22*

According to the gospels, relating eyewitness accounts of the life of Jesus, he spoke often of his death, burial, and resurrection before it occurred. The evidence shows Jesus knew he would be raised from the dead.

Second, many witnessed his trial, crucifixion, and burial. All four gospels record the trial of Jesus. Secular history also mentions this event. A crucifixion involved a severe beating before placement on a cross. Some victims died from the beating alone. Suffocation usually brought death to the person crucified.

Alive after being placed on the cross according to Gospel accounts, the Roman soldiers noted Jesus' death while he hung there. The blood and water that poured from his side when pierced shows he not only lost consciousness, but truly died. The mixture of blood and pericardial fluid (water) is a sign of death.

The gospel of John adds, *"The soldiers therefore came and broke the legs of the first man who had been crucified with Jesus, and then those of the other. But when they came to Jesus and found that he was already dead, they did not break his legs. Instead one of the soldiers pierced Jesus' side with a spear, bringing a sudden flow of blood and water." John 19:32-34*

Evidence of death and burial is clear in the gospels. Followers wrapped Jesus' body in the traditional way and placed it in a rock tomb. Then a large stone, rolled into place, sealed the tomb. Logic dictates Jesus, suffering from the beating and hours on the cross and wrapped in such cloths, even if still alive when placed in the tomb, could not move such a large stone to free himself. Any courtroom summation would stress the evidence shows Jesus' death and burial.

The Easter story tells of the women coming to the tomb on Sunday morning and finding it empty, the stone rolled away. This brings us to the third point of the legal case. Witnesses who saw Jesus after the resurrection.

Many eyewitnesses testified to seeing the living Jesus. He walked among them, ate with them, and talked to them. The gospels' most dramatic testimony indicates Jesus invited Thomas to place his fingers on his wounds and told him to stop doubting. The written records show as many as five hundred eye witnesses saw Jesus after his death on the cross. Acts 1:3, Matthew 28:9-10,

Mark 16:14, Luke 24:13-31 and 38-39, John 20:19-29 and John 21, I Corinthians 15:1-8.

Opposing counsel may offer the explanation the Romans or Jews stole Jesus' body. The natural rebuttal? Why didn't they show the body and parade it around for all to see, exposing these Jesus followers as frauds.

Also, how could the cowardly disciples, afraid to show themselves at Jesus' crucifixion, become convinced of the resurrection to the point they began to tell others with a passion and conviction unseen in the history of the world? Why would they risk their lives by testifying to a lie?

Many Christian martyrs gave their lives for their belief in the resurrected Jesus. Imagine the strength of one's conviction to cling to this idea, even to the point of death. Our study of Paul's life and adventures also dictates a strong, personal belief in the living Jesus. Otherwise, why suffer the troubles Paul endured? There is no logical answer other than these Christians knew Jesus lives.

When teens ask me whether I believe in the physical resurrection of Jesus, I demur by saying my thoughts are not important, what they think is most important. I go on to point out my lawyer's training sees much evidence to show Jesus rose from the dead; his predictions of death and resurrection, eye witness accounts of the trial, crucifixion, and death, and finally, the eye witness testimony of seeing, being with, and interacting with Jesus in the days following his death.

I concluded my argument by saying even if we don't know how the physical resurrection could occur, *something happened* at that particular time and place to start what we now call Christianity.

The idea of a living Jesus can enrich our lives today, but each of us gets to decide what we believe.

Oh, the young woman who thought the resurrection story must be a myth or legend? She graduated nursing school with honors and works pediatrics at a large metropolitan hospital. Patients under her care receive a blessing by having such a woman caring for them. Another one for the accomplished list.

CHAPTER EIGHTEEN

What Does God Look Like to You?

Let us play word association. I say a word and you tell me what images pop into your mind.

"God."

"Uh, tall guy with long robe and beard, maybe holding some stone commandments"?

That would be Moses, but at least it makes a good start.

As we saw with the idea of Jesus' resurrection, reconciling faith and reason is a hard sell, especially to know-it-all teens who often expound on the latest thing they read or learned. Learning scientific theories and concepts empower them but can reveal skepticism under the surface.

They may not articulate the difference between secular humanism—a naturalistic worldview with an emotional thrust in a positive ethical outlook—and atheism, which they understand as a belief in no God and no ethics, but they form certain beliefs at this age.

While this view of atheism is not entirely accurate, it reflects the thinking of many teens. From their science classes, they know cause and effect from the scientific method, but putting all of this together with one's faith is difficult. Welcome to the real world.

Many do not know the term Christian Apologist—one who explains and defends the faith against doubters—but they seek answers to the same questions many of us have and look for someone to fill the role.

I am a big supporter of helping teens learn to think for themselves. I do not favor dictating what they should believe. I consider it an honor should they call me a Christian Apologist, not afraid to pose the big, difficult questions of Christianity and participate in a robust discussion.

Teens, like the rest of us, struggle getting their minds around the concept of God. Understanding this, I figured we could spend a year, or most of one, discussing how we viewed God, and what difference our image of God makes to our religious experience. This is the short version of how we looked at the Images of God idea.

To begin, we covered some basics. Cokesbury, the official publisher of United Methodist Church publications, issued a Confirmation Teaching Aid with twelve completing phrases for the statement: God is . . .

We used this as a starting point for our discussions:

First, God is One. The United Methodist Church teaches this principle. The Power behind all, beyond all, and within all is one—not many. Our creed echoes the basic creed of the Jewish faith as well: *"Hear, O Israel: the Lord our God, the Lord is one." Mark 12:29*

Methodists also believe in the trinity, God is Three in One. We identify the name God as three persons: God the Father, God the Son (Jesus Christ), and God the Spirit (Holy Spirit). These are not three separate beings, but different expressions of the same one God in perfect relationship with one another. We call this understanding the Trinity.

We also believe God is the Source of All There Is, the source of everything. Whatever exists came from God. God is the creative force in and behind it all. This confirms *Genesis 1:1 "In the beginning . . . God . . ."*

We discussed how United Methodists believe God is the Sustaining Power of the Universe. God does not take vacations. God did not start the universe and then retire. God is the sustaining presence within the universe. We believe looking into the vastness of the galaxies or recognizing the wonder of atoms and subatomic particles, is beholding God.

Methodists also believe God is Eternal. God always has been and always will be. No time existed before God or without God. God is the Alpha and Omega, the beginning and the end, the first and the last. In singing our "Gloria Patri—Glory be to the Father"—we affirm God as eternal "as it was in the beginning, is now, and ever shall be."

We also touched on how Methodists believe God is Holy. We believe God is set apart, perfect, filled with unlimited love, and worthy of awe. The Bible speaks of this dimension as God's holiness, which is a quality unique to the nature of God. God's holiness demands holiness from us as well, even though we cannot achieve it. God's sanctifying grace draws us towards holiness. We call persons or places holy because they are set apart and marked by God's nature in a special way.

The teens who went through confirmation class knew these principles and discussed them easily. We did not take a vote, but most of the class agreed these tenets matched their beliefs.

Some expressed impatience I touched on things they already knew, so after the first time through the subject, to avoid being pedantic or doctrinaire, I broke the topic half way through and jumped into other discussion topics.

Growing up in a family with a patriarch who served as a district judge gave me some familiarity with authority figures. As many perceive her, God is perhaps the largest authority figure of all time.

I read somewhere classic Arabic contains ninety-nine words for Allah/God. English demonstrates an ability to expand even more. One clever exposition put four words or phrases together and came up with over 25 million portrayals of God: Active-Affirming-Architect-Of All, Fiery-Empowering-Engineer-Of the Faithful, Merciful-Judging-Mentor-Of Reality, Triumphant-Saving-Source-Of Joy. You get the idea, an almost never-ending list of ways to conceive God.

Did you ever hear a child ask, "Who made God?"

I experienced this and struggled to give a cogent answer to a six-year-old. Teens exhibit better logic and reasoning skills than six-year-olds, but wrestle with the same concepts. Some of this comes from the cosmological thought process. Simply put, we explain the world or cosmos as things in the physical universe; those we see, touch, hear, and think. The physical universe is dependent on these things. What exists, to this line of thinking, has a cause or reason for its existence. We figure it is impossible for any one thing to produce itself. Relating causes to effects allows us to trace the universe back through a succession, hence the cosmologists' Big Bang theory. Of course, the kids then ask, "What caused the Big Bang?" and you find yourself right back where you started. Human minds strive to conceive something beyond this.

Following this line of thought gets us back to something, but not a cause. What is the external cause for the universe we see and measure? Nothing? The puzzle; nothing cannot produce something, at least to our thinking.

Atheists use this dead end of reasoning to say there is no something beyond. There is no God, if you will. Others, I included, reason there must be something, and we conceive a deity, a God, something carrying the reason of existence within itself. This search for a necessary thing or *causa sui*, Latin for cause of itself, puzzled humans for ages. Talk about a leap of faith! There it is.

You heard the one about the child who announced he would draw a picture of God. His Father says, "No one knows what God looks like" and the child responds, "They will as soon as I finish this picture." Maybe this infantile certainty helps us with this dilemma.

We try to use means to an end thinking to get a grip on our image of God. Throughout nature, we apply design, thought, wisdom, and our intelligence to form productions in our mind, all of human contrivance. The argument by analogy is the world resembles the objects of human design, but the Bible tells us the heavens and the earth declare the glory of God. Therein lies the answer for me.

Maybe what we see and know of the heavens and earth are only human constructions in our minds. Allowing ourselves to admit God is unfathomable, beyond our reasoning, and exceeds the capability of the human mind, provides another avenue for thinking about this. If God is beyond our reasoning, what do we have to provide a human concept of God? Luckily, our experience and the Bible provide many suggestions. Those suggestions became the basis for our study.

We discussed some of those images. The class participated quickly and offered some of their own ideas. Many related to political leadership—King, Judge, Ruler, and Lord. Others related to everyday human existence—builder, gardener, shepherd, potter, doctor, healer, mother, father, lover, wise man, friend, and woman giving birth. Still others related to natural and inanimate objects—eagle, lion, bear, hen, fire, light, cloud, breath, rock, fortress, shield, and the Word. These got us started, but we added more thoughts to the exercise.

What do these word pictures evoke in us? Citizens of modern America lack practical experience with a King, but we know enough stories from literature, history, and the Bible to ground us with the image. A King shows grandeur, majesty, glory as reflected by a palace, a court, clothing, crown—especially when compared to common people. A King is the central authority for the kingdom, one where only the means available limit his power. A King is often a Judge and Lawgiver, the source and enforcer of the law, the source of order within the kingdom, one who provides order to chaos, and possibly a creator—one who made the kingdom possible. A King can also provide justice and an ideal King can treat everyone fairly, a champion of justice for all.

We took the discussion one-step further by examining the effects produced by this model or picture of God. God as King or Judge creates the idea God is distant and separate from us. Closeness to a Lawgiver/Judge is a tough one. Being at one with this thought simply does not compute for most of us. The image also focuses on sin and guilt. Disobeying the law brings punishment. The ideas of mercy, forgiveness, a second chance, probably do not fit here. This idea conjures thoughts about meeting the requirements, obeying the law, and measuring up to the standard.

I believe this creates a performance model for us. We must perform or do something to gain God's love. I told the class I believed this contradicted Paul's pronouncement we are justified by our faith. Following the Pharisee's idea of "the law, the law, and the law" is not enough to gain God's love. We do not do things to deserve God's love; it is just there for us. We cannot earn it. It is there for the asking. It is grace.

These ideas brought great discussions with the class as to their image of God. They also showed how our concept could grow and expand as we study and mature.

What about the natural or inanimate things? A fire can represent comfort, safety and warmth, but also danger and destruction. I heard a Southern Baptist preacher tell me the sinners would "fry like sausages when they reached Hell." I preferred not to dwell on the idea with the class. A fire can be a purifying agent, one separating precious metals from ore, not one to destroy only. Using it as a threat or cudgel to get one to believe in God does not fit my theology.

Fire as light in the darkness, a guide/beacon to show the way, a source of safety and protection; these are all benevolent images for us. Fire is also mysterious; it flickers, is ethereal, and exhibits the duality of life giving and life destroying simultaneously. These thoughts bounced around our discussions.

We later added categories for the different ways we see God. These included anthropomorphic, non-anthropomorphic, those showing closeness, those exhibiting distance, and ones of gender.

Anthropomorphic is a word not totally familiar to teens, but one lady in class told me she felt smart because she encountered this word on her Scholastic Aptitude Test study words. Turned out she actually learned something in Sunday school to help her in high school. Go figure.

We talked about humanlike or anthropomorphic images of God. We also presented animals, things, elements—thoughts of non-humanlike concepts. The closeness/distance discussion generated many comments and a few revelations of how this line of thinking opened them to new ways of looking at God.

My experiences with a father who served as a judge expanded the conversation. I saw him not only as an authority figure who decided things and determined punishment, but also as one who loved me and showed mercy, kindness, and forgiveness. He sat behind a bench in an elevated position above all others in the courtroom and they showed deference. These experiences also tied into the idea of closeness and distance inferred from an idea or portrayal. This helped some see the many ways these images can work.

The gender concepts produced some excited discussions. The women loved the concept of seeing God as a woman. More than one repeated the bumper sticker phrase: "God is coming, and is SHE pissed." Some read the popular novel *The Shack*, where God appears as a black woman, and liked the thought. Most males showed indifference, some open hostility to the idea God could be a woman. We at least got full participation in the discussion.

Working through these straightforward mental images took several weeks and held the class' attention. I believed this helped us broaden our concepts of God and how we might relate to those concepts.

God as a spirit presented an alternative picture harder for many to see. This stressed the relationship, intimacy, and belonging to a non-material reality. We talked about Pentecost when God sent the Holy Spirit and how the early Christians wrote of their experiences. "Tongues of fire descending from heaven" gets downright Biblical but forces us to adjust our thinking.

Now when the Day of Pentecost came, they were all together in one place. Suddenly a sound like the blowing of a violent wind came from heaven and filled the whole house where they were sitting. They saw what seemed to be tongues of fire, that separated and came to rest on each of them. All of them were filled with the Holy Spirit and began to speak in other tongues, as the Spirit enabled them. Acts 2:1–4

There you have noise, wind, and fire—all symbolic of God's spirit. The class got the idea the early Christians felt something happening; something so startling they needed to record it.

God as spirit turned out so fertile, we used spirit for another set of classes and discussions. This also opened great discussions about how we can experience God's presence in us and God's engagement with the world. The class related many experiences they called "God things," when circumstances, coincidences, and so on, came together in their lives. Some were mundane—how they passed a math quiz without studying and others sacred—when someone appeared at a crucial time in their lives and helped them through grief, pain, fear, and other difficult situations.

We read about the Hebrew word *ruach*, which means wind and/or spirit, as a description of the Holy Spirit. Wind or a breeze is invisible, but manifestly real, and something to which all of us could relate. This helped us see what often comes only through faith.

It also presented an opportunity to extol the wisdom of Paul who in *Hebrews 11:1 wrote, "Now faith is being sure of what we hope for and certain of what we do not see."* We hope for a relationship with God even though we cannot see God and have a difficult time articulating the concept.

Next, we got to gender. If God is truly a spirit, what does God need with gender? Male/female/neither/both? This concept can apply to a spirit more than to the anthropomorphic images we discussed earlier. Spirit transcends the boundaries that come with anthropomorphic and non-anthropomorphic figures.

We talked about the effects of this Spirit model of God. How does it affect our thinking? It gives us great insight by emphasizing the nearness/closeness of God and presupposes we can have a connection to her. We can have a relationship with this representation of God. The idea allows us to live within the Spirit or vice versa, the Spirit lives within us.

The class liked the idea somehow, we live within God and God lives within us. The image also allowed transcendence—a recognition of something more than metaphors or buzzwords for God. Now we were getting somewhere, and we called upon some input from a former class member, Janos, as we moved to more discussion about God as Spirit.

CHAPTER NINETEEN

An Infinite Fish Tank

How do different images change our perception of God?

The idea started getting us into some deep theological threads. This made me wish I attended seminary instead of law school. Too late for that. Reading and studying on my own added some depth to my reasoning, but I owe much to a bunch of teenagers meeting on Sunday mornings nine months out of the year.

God as Spirit? The idea provides food for thought. I believe the last 200 hundred years or so brought us a trend toward a logical, rational thought process and away from manifestations of the Spirit.

Many mainstream Protestant churches exhibited a pattern of denial or de-emphasis of the Pentecost call or made an effort to ignore it completely. Beginning in the late 1800s and throughout the 1900s, our society and many churches took prevalent ideas of science and replaced spirit in religion with those ideas.

John Wesley, as the founder, and Charles Wesley, an early devotee to what we call Methodism, saw the presence of the Spirit in themselves and the movement they promoted, but while some churches emphasized the Spirit, others, and to me this includes the United Methodist Church, did not. (Read *Subversive Fire: The Untold Story of Pentecost,* Albert Hernandez, Emeth Press, 2010)

In class we talked about some Pentecostal and/or Evangelical churches where people spoke in tongues, went into trances, or handled snakes, all under the guise of the Holy Spirit. Some teens experienced worship services like this and were quick to comment on them. Most liked the enthusiastic singing and music they deemed Spirit led but lacked an overall comfort level with such worship services.

We talked about how different people experience God in different ways and how we need to be careful not to denigrate the beliefs of others. I told them how my view needed each of us to decide what he or she believes and how we experience God, and that is a good thing. I sincerely doubt I know all the ways God manifests herself and I found myself uncomfortable dismissing someone's experiences as wrong or inappropriate.

But, what about the idea of God as Spirit? How can we live within the Spirit or vice versa, the Spirit lives within us? The class merely liking this idea left us a long way from grasping the deeper meaning or transcendence of it. How can we effectively talk about God as Spirit?

I mentioned this discussion in a letter to Janos Toevs. As usual, he wrote several things, and I shared them with the class:

My word association to God is first, Truth. Not as in Gospel truth, but as in "the truth is like God," it doesn't require you to believe in it to be real.

The image that comes with the word 'God' is an infinite fish tank. Odd, but consider this. When I discuss faith and religion with people, I ask, "So, do you realize God is as much a part of you as you are of him?" Some people have a hard time with this concept because they think of infinite as a linear abstraction—the line with arrows at each end indicating it goes on forever in both directions. But an infinite being, entity, whatever, would be on all dimensions, not only linear extension. So, I say, "Imagine the universe as a fish tank. We, as people, are the fish in the tank. God? God is the water. He is all around us and in us. He is part of us and we are part of him."

Because the truth is infinite in all dimensions, even time, this truth is not only part of time and space it transcends it. So, if God is infinite and the truth is infinite, then my philosophical search for the truth is a search for God. And, every truth I understand and embrace is an understanding and embracing of God. And when through asceticism or introspection, I discover truth in myself, like "Man is at his best when pursuing a goal and inevitably begins to decline once he attains it." That is finding God in me. Whether God as Truth, or God as my ability to articulate things, a God-given talent; or God as in sharing something of value, maybe even something priceless, with no expectation or even desire for reciprocity, it is God!

Wow! Many of us expanded our minds to grasp the infinite fish tank idea. Several used the example later when we discussed the concept of the Holy Spirit being God within us and us living through this Spirit. One woman returned from a mission trip around the world, touching down in eleven countries over eleven months, and told me she took this image with her. Pretty cool image of God we got from Janos, a high school dropout, serving time for murder.

Looking back at the fundamental teachings of the United Methodist Church allowed us to continue this Spirit line of thinking and then jump to other ideas of God. The United Methodist Church teaches God is Spirit. Although God is present within creation, God is not a physical object located in time and space. God is present in all creation, as our presence comes in all parts of our body at the same time. And, as we are more than our bodies, so, too, God transcends the universe. This spirit, not a thing or object, garners emphasis in our faith. We speak of God as the Holy Spirit living within each of us.

The Church tells us God is personal. This holy, transcendent God is also approachable. God is a being, a being who seeks a relationship with us, invites us into a relationship, and invites us to draw ever closer. One of the ways Christians experience this personal God is through Jesus Christ. Many of the more devout class members agreed with this characterization. We also believe God is present with us. God is holy and unlike us in many respects, but God is not distant. God is present in our world and in our lives. We can pray to God, talk to God, listen to God, receive guidance by God, and enjoy a relationship with God.

The United Methodists believe God is redeemer. God is not neutral. God cares. God wants us to be in right relationship with God, and God acts to make it possible to redeem or set right again our relationship. *"For God so loved the world that he gave his one and only Son (Jesus Christ)." John 3:16*

We believe God is proactive, reaching out to us and inviting us back to God. We believe God is Love. More than anything else, God is love. God cares. God forgives. God seeks us out. God desires a relationship of love with us. Loving is God's vision for creation.

Laying out the basics of Methodism allowed us to focus on what we believed, but it also drew us into discussions of what we did not believe. Between 1984 and 2017, my time leading this class, our society saw many advancements in scientific learning. How our schools taught scientific principles also received challenges. The kids saw this and deemed it a subject for our discussion on how we view God.

Many fundamental Christians, believing in the literal interpretation of the Bible, oppose other views, especially evolution of the species by natural selection. This viewpoint often turned political during the years I taught Sunday school. While often conflated with other political views, it played out in public schools across America. The State of Colorado held several school board elections highlighting this issue and the state legislature looked at the availability of charter schools in more districts. Some saw the charter school issue as a straw man for Creationism or this fundamental view of Christianity.

Creationism is defined as a doctrine or theory holding God created matter, the various forms of life, and the world, out of nothing, usually in the way described in Genesis. Or, put another way, the belief the universe and living organisms originate from specific acts of divine creation, as in the biblical account, rather than by natural processes such as evolution. Creationism can be another term for creation science.

Many websites exist with scads of literature on both sides of this issue and many teens read them and wanted to discuss the ideas presented. One such site, *Creationism.org*, exhorts its readers to become active in the discussion.

On the first page of the website, I read the following: "*Each new false religion of the post-Flood period has sought to detract from our creator and from our responsibilities in this life; evolution's effect is no different and it (macro-evolution) continues to lack any scientific substance. Pray about this! And study as needed, especially since the media continues to report this issue inaccurately. Please study the plethora of Biblical and scientific knowledge standing squarely against this spiritual deception.*"

Of course, this view conflicts with generally accepted scientific views. Before long, the matter got into our classroom, and of course, I became the first target.

"Hey, Charlie, I read I can't be a Christian and believe in evolution. Is that true?" One Sunday, a class member offered this before I could start our lesson. It grabbed the class's interest, so we scrapped our planned lesson and got into a long discussion.

My first inclination, passing or ignoring the issue, went against my instincts. I tried to think how we could get into this without hurting someone's feelings or sounding elitist, or condescending. My liberal view might go against the views of some conservative classmates. I remembered the early advice I received about working with teens. "Be yourself. They can spot phonies a mile away." Soon, we were deep into it and I knew no choice but to put my views before the class.

"Well, I believe you can be a Christian and believe in evolution," I began. "I don't believe humans in our present form were created in the past 10,000 years and evolution played no part. I agree with the scientific consensus human beings evolved from less advanced forms of life over millions of years, and I certainly do not think this makes me an atheist. I believe we can have science and faith. To me, evolution can be God's way of creating life on Earth. I believe God is still working on me. Why can't she be working on all humans?"

I told the class the lawyer in me wished for a role like Clarence Darrow's representing the defense in the famous Scopes Monkey Trial of 1925. The case involved a science teacher accused of violating Tennessee law by teaching evolution. A law, in my view, based upon religious bigotry. I forcefully stated religious bigotry is still bigotry and I do not think God likes it. I told them I fully supported the United Methodist Church tag line Open Hearts, Open Minds, Open Doors to illustrate its policy of allowing different points of view within the body of the church. If people of faith cannot discuss these issues, we are all in trouble.

I continued by saying, "Put me down on the religious liberal side. I do not favor teaching creationism in public schools or having the government support a museum about Noah's ark. I will not take a Christian tour of the Grand Canyon where the tour guide tries to convince me everything I see happened in the last 8,000 years. I refuse to believe this timeline for our world or that we face an either/or proposition between faith and science. The God I believe in can do all things; even use evolutionary processes to get it done. To think otherwise, to me, is too narrow a view of God. Some people call this idea Divine evolution and I like the idea."

This raised a few eyebrows, but no one left the room. Some nodded, at least in tacit agreement. I wondered how long before I received calls from parents or the senior pastor asked me in for a sit-down discussion of what goes on in the high school class. Luckily, the day never came, and I continued to relate essentially the same view in future classes.

I also believe God's image can come to us in many ways. The Old Testament is replete with stories of God appearing to folks in dreams or visions. I have not experienced this but know many have. I cannot doubt their sincerity. If God is an unsurpassable being or a being beyond conceivable improvement, as Anselm posited, then surely God can come to us in many ways, forms, and methods.

A few years after he graduated our class, one of our classmates, became trapped in a slot canyon in a remote area of Utah, and faced an agonizing death by shock, exposure, and dehydration. After days in this desperate situation, he carved an epitaph into the sandstone walls of the canyon, stating his name, the month of his birth and the month of his rapidly approaching death. He leaned back in his backpack harness, his right hand and wrist trapped by a boulder against the canyon wall and slipped into a trance.

Color filled his vision as he walked from the canyon into a living room. He saw a blond, three-year-old boy in a red polo shirt, running toward him and he scooped to pick him up with his left arm, used his handless right arm to balance the boy, and they laughed together. They smiled, pranced around the room and the boy giggled as they twirled together. He intuitively knew this image as his son. Suddenly, the vison blacked out and he found himself back in the canyon, trapped as before. But, he felt reassured he would survive his entrapment.

He thrashed back and forth with his body against the canyon wall and lost his composure, frustrated at his predicament.

BETWEEN A ROCK
AND A HARD PLACE
ARON
RALSTON

Then, he felt his arm bend in an unnatural way, pinned by the boulder holding his wrist and forearm against the stone. Suddenly, his motion stopped. An idea came to him. If he torqued his arm far enough, he could break the bones, cut through the flesh, and free himself.

He proceeded and broke free from the boulder and the canyon wall. While severely injured, he scrambled out of the canyon. Before he met others to help, he executed a forty-foot rappel to the canyon floor with his right arm bound in a slap-dash tourniquet to stanch the loss of blood from his self-amputation. Long story short, Aron Ralston gets a helicopter rescue to medical assistance and proceeds with a months' long rehabilitation. (Read *Between a Rock and a Hard Place*, Aron Ralston, Atria Books, 2004)

I believe Aron received an image of God in the vision of a three-year-old boy he knew to be his son. To me, this image came from God. The image helped reassure him in a time of dire danger. Ultimately, actions spurred by the vision, allowed him to reach safety and continue a productive life.

Aron Ralston, a father, motivational and self-help speaker, best-selling author, world traveler, mountain climber, skier, and modern-day explorer of God's natural beauty; definitely one for the A list.

CHAPTER TWENTY

Accomplished or Under Construction Thirty-Three Years of Blessings

In 1984, my adventure with teens started with trepidation and anxiety. When the senior pastor asked me to teach a Sunday school class for teenagers, I felt wholly inadequate and unprepared for the task. At the time, I thought the pastor wanted my time and effort, but he actually wanted to give me a gift. I looked at the proposal from my self-centered perspective with no idea what the future held. The unexpected conversations with teenagers over the next thirty-three years enriched me, challenged me, and ultimately made me a better person.

Those years went quickly and now looking back, I realize what a blessing he offered me. The encounter with the pastor literally changed my life for the good. Some find it improbable one person and one day can change your life, but I know this can happen.

All of the individuals listed below shared a classroom with me during parts of thirty-three years. Some came and went quickly, only appearing once or twice in class. Others spent most Sundays with me over a four-year period of our lives. All influenced me.

The accomplished or A list:

An associate pastor of a large Presbyterian church in a major U.S. city.

An award-winning teacher loved by students and colleagues alike.

A physician working tirelessly to heal and lessen suffering for patients.

A business executive recognized by Forbes magazine as one of 30 Outstanding Professionals under the Age of 30.

Assorted professionals: Engineers, Attorneys, Architects, Nurses, CPAs, Salespersons, Consultants.

A U. S. Army officer responsible for the well-being of over 300 servicemen and women.

An executive director of a Homeless Shelter and HIV/AIDS Clinic in San Francisco, California.

A nationally known outdoorsman/adventurer, motivational and self-help speaker.

Those on the under construction list:

An alcoholic and drug abuser unable to hold a job.

A teenaged son and daughter estranged from parents and family.

A sixteen-year-old unwed mother and father.

A seventeen-year-old thief, serving a two-year probation for breaking and entering a private residence.

A sixteen-year-old on probation for illegal possession of firearms, involved with a Wiccan cult in Indiana.

An eighteen-year-old suffering from opioid addiction.

A twenty-year-old sentenced to life in prison for murder.

Most of us are familiar with those on the first list. Those are our kind of folks—successful, educated, responsible, living lives of value to society. Don't we all aspire to be on the accomplished list?

The under construction list? Do we know those folks? Or, do we admit we know those folks, or are those folks? They are troubled, misguided, lost children, having a difficult time relating to the norms of our culture and society. I prefer to exhibit the Christian principles of forgiveness and redemption when looking at those on the list. No one is beyond Christ's love, especially teens under construction. And, rather than feel conceit for those on the accomplished list, I believe we all, upon reflection can say, "*There, but for the grace of God, go I.*"

Years ago, my sister died in an automobile accident on a Friday evening. We got the news late at night and left for Texas early the next morning to be with my family. Before leaving, I notified our church pastor. Despite the early hour, she said "I will be right there." She did not say I need to fix my hair, chose suitable clothes, or have my coffee first, she showed the love and concern for others (me) by saying she would come at once. I rejoiced knowing she led our community of faith.

I told her that was not necessary, we were ready to begin our drive. She prayed with us over the phone and gave her blessing for our family. I mentioned I would not lead the class on Sunday morning and she agreed to take care of finding a substitute.

My substitute received little warning and nothing from me to help but proved up to the task. The senior high group wrote letters to me during the class. I treasure those letters and they warm my heart each time I re-read them. They expressed sympathy, compassion, and love for me. Even though the class did not know my sister, they knew me, and that provided enough incentive. Without my interaction with those teens, no such blessing occurs.

Author, far right, with youth mission team - Carlsbad Caverns, NM

Over three decades I laughed on many occasions, cried on more than I preferred, and I hope, mentored young people about growing into the modern world. We enjoyed great moments of joy and endured heartbreaking moments of grief and sadness. I saw them grow from gangly, acne marked, socially inept young people into strong, faithful, competent, and fully functioning adults who contribute to a better world. Of course, like all of us, some are still under construction.

Some may recall the hilarious Gary Larson cartoon, *The Far Side*. His work included humorous looks at bizarre and improbable events in our world. Many animals appeared but found themselves in human-like conditions. The cartoons often referred to awkward social settings and a search for deeper meaning. In some ways, I saw interaction with teenagers as a trip to the far side, but over time, I came to realize teens occupy a realm not so far from the adult world. Sure, their brains are not fully developed and their recognition patterns still need maturity, but upon close examination, teens resemble us all. In my judgment, adults are not much different from teenagers. As Pogo says in the famous Walt Kelly cartoon, "We have met the enemy, and he is us!" I look at my adventures with teens under construction as a trip to the not so far side.

I believe the youth of Hope United Methodist Church in Greenwood Village, Colorado are not much different from the youth of most towns in America. My experiences gave me confidence in future generations and an expectation of being surprised as new teenagers mature. Of course, some will stumble and fall. They may appear on an under construction list, at least for a while, but we can grow and learn from them all. We can also love them and be patient.

As the scripture says, "If a man owns a hundred sheep, and one of them wanders away, will he not leave the ninety-nine on the hills and go to look for the one that wandered off? And if he finds it, truly I tell you, he is happier about that one sheep than about the ninety-nine that did not wander off."

I know the mission is to avoid any lost sheep; and, as all Marines become dedicated to the mission, I hope all people of faith take on this mission. I fervently believe this is not only a job for a youth pastor or the parents of teenagers, but for all of us. God will rejoice as one comes off the under-construction list, as should we all.

How can we help? For all teenagers we meet; acknowledge them, encourage them, and love them. What can you expect for the effort? Blessings beyond your imagining.

About the Author

Charles C. "Charlie" Ledbetter recently retired from a legal and consulting career spanning over forty years. As a national business leader for one of the world's largest benefits consulting firms during the last fourteen years of his career, Charlie directed a team of consultants advising clients on legal, accounting, compliance, and investing matters relating to 401(k) retirement plans.

As the Trail Boss for the Ledbetter Land & Cattle Company, Charlie is an accomplished public speaker, consultant to businesses, and emerging author/publisher of nonfiction memoirs.

An avid reader and volunteer, he holds a B. A. in history from Baylor University and a Juris Doctor degree from the Sturm College of Law at the University of Denver.

Charlie is a life-long United Methodist and member of Hope United Methodist Church in Greenwood Village, Colorado where he taught senior high Sunday school for thirty-three years, served as the church historian, and received the Sam Day Award for outstanding volunteer service to his church. He served eleven years on the board of directors for the United Methodist Foundation for the Rocky Mountain Conference, recently serving as the chair of the Investment Committee.

Charlie is married, lives in Denver, Colorado near his two sons, enjoys attending the varied activities of his four grandchildren, and is an avid photographer. He has traveled extensively; visiting five continents and twenty-six countries worldwide.